PRAYING THE
NEW TESTAMENT
AS PSALMS

All Christian living is founded on prayer, and that prayer has a particular focus when it is grounded in Holy Scripture. Because prayer is an encounter with God, it is something that transcends denominational boundaries, and I am sure that *Praying the New Testament as Psalms* will be a useful resource for all Christians, helping them to encounter the New Testament in new a creative ways. I warmly recommend it.

George Carey
Archbishop of Canterbury, England

In this book of prayers the authors have shared their splendid, complementary gifts with the readers. Prayer is sometimes described as "life with the living God." The user of *Praying the New Testament as Psalms* will find guidance, nourishment and grace for life in this inspiring book.

Francis George
Cardinal Archbishop of Chicago

Praying the New Testament as Psalms is a different kind of prayer book. Totally scriptural, it is therefore direct, deep and full of feeling but devoid of sentimentality. It will help the Spirit to pray through us "according to the will of God" (Rom 8:27).

Ronald Rolheiser
Author of The Holy Longing

PRAYING THE NEW TESTAMENT AS PSALMS

Desmond O'Donnell
Maureen Mohen

ASSISTING CHRISTIANS TO ACT
PUBLICATIONS

Praying the New Testament as Psalms
by Desmond O'Donnell, OMI, and Maureen Mohen, RSM

Father Desmond O'Donnell is a member of the Oblate community in Ireland, of which he has been General Counselor for twelve years. He is an internationally known author, lecturer and retreat director. Sister Maureen Mohen is a member of the Sisters of Mercy in Australia. She is a musician, teacher and pastoral minister and has produced a number of worship resources.

Cover design by Tom A. Wright
Typesetting by Desktop Edit Shop, Inc.

Originally published in Ireland by Veritas Publications as *Psalming the New Testament.* Copyright © 2002 by Desmond O'Donnell.

Scripture quotations are from the New Revised Standard Version of the Bible, copyright © 1989 by the Division of Christian Education of the National Council of the Churches of Christ in the U.S.A. Used with permission. All rights reserved.

The authors acknowledge use of *Theological Dictionary of the New Testament* by Geoffrey W. Bromley (Eerdman), *Expository Dictionary of Bible Words* by Lawrence Richards (Regency), and *The Life Application Bible* (Tyndale Publishers) for insight and inspiration.

Published by: ACTA Publications
          Assisting Christians To Act
          4848 N. Clark Street
          Chicago, IL 60640-4711
          773-271-1030

Library of Congress Catalog Number: 2002104340
ISBN: 0-87946-233-7
Printed in the United States of America
Printing: 10 9 8 7 6 5 4 3 2 1
Year: 08 07 06 05 04 03 02

CONTENTS

Preface / 9

Beatitudes (Luke) / 12
Beatitudes (Matthew) / 14
Blessing / 16
Body / 18
Celebration / 20
Christ – Authority / 22
Christ – Human / 24
Christ – Icon of God / 26
Christ – King / 28
Christ – Liberator / 30
Christ – Messiah / 32
Christ – Mystery / 34
Christ – Obedient / 36
Christ – Praying / 38
Christ – God's Word / 40
Christ – Shepherd / 42
Christ – Suffering / 44
Compassion / 46
Conscience / 48
Covenant / 50
Co-Workers with God / 52
Death / 54
Detachment / 56
Discernment / 58
Discipleship / 60
Ecology / 62
Encouragement / 64
Endurance / 66
Eucharist / 68
Faith / 70
Family / 72
Fatherhood / 74
Fellowship / 76

Forgiveness / 78
Freedom / 80
Friendship / 82
Fruit / 84
Glory / 86
God's Love / 88
God in All / 90
Gratitude / 92
Healing / 94
Heart / 96
Holiness / 98
Holy Spirit / 100
Hope / 102
Hospitality / 104
Immortality / 106
John the Baptizer / 108
Joseph / 110
Journey of Life / 112
Joy / 114
Kingdom / 116
Leadership / 118
Life / 120
Light / 122
Listening / 124
Loving God / 126
Magdalene / 128
Marriage / 130
Mary / 132
Meals / 134
Mercy / 136
Miracle / 138
Mission / 140
Motherhood / 142
Obedience / 144
Patience / 146
Paul / 148
Peace / 150
Perseverance / 152

Peter / 154

Possessions / 156

Prayer / 158

Purity of Heart / 160

Reconciliation / 162

Redemption / 164

Repentance / 166

Resurrection / 168

Sacrifice / 170

Salvation / 172

Self-Transcendence / 174

Sharing / 176

Sin / 178

Sincerity / 180

Social Justice / 182

Suffering / 184

Temptation / 186

Trinity / 188

Truth / 190

Union with God / 192

Victory / 194

Waiting / 196

Water / 198

Weakness / 200

Wisdom / 202

Witness / 204

Woman / 206

Word / 208

Worship / 210

Index / 212

PREFACE

After two millennia of Christianity, there isn't much that can truly be said to be "new" in using the Scriptures as a starting place for personal or collective prayer. But in *Praying the New Testament as Psalms,* Desmond O'Donnell and Maureen Mohen have created an innovative approach to the New Testament that makes the texts come alive in unexpected and delight-filled ways.

Using the couplet form of the ancient Hebrew psalms, the authors have developed 100 new psalms based on the New Testament. Each psalm is composed around a specific thought or theme. By paraphrasing and juxtaposing verses from the four gospels, the various epistles, the Acts of the Apostles and the Book of Revelation, Father O'Donnell and Sister Mohen have provided a fresh way of experiencing the New Testament texts.

Like the psalms of the Hebrew Scriptures, these "New Testament psalms" are meant to raise minds and hearts to God. They differ greatly in language, based as they are on different writers and parts of the New Testament. Some are poetic in their rhythm and style, others are relatively prosaic, although still filled with great feeling and truth.

Scriptural references for each psalm are carefully noted, and the index lists where specific New Testament verses or passages are cited. The reader can begin with a certain theme presented alphabetically in the table of contents and allow that theme to suggest others. The book can also be opened and prayed at random in a *lectio divina* style.

The guiding principle should be flexibility. These psalms can be prayed in any sequence, and likewise the individual verses within each psalm can be prayed in different order. It is not necessary to read each psalm from "top to bottom." Letting the eye fall as it will, allowing the different nuances and emphases to interact, will deepen appreciation of the theme as a whole. Each psalm is self-contained and deserves individual and repeated contemplation. Going back to the New Testament to read the referenced verses in their context will also enhance reflection on these psalms.

If the book is used for group prayer, the psalms can be proclaimed by a lector or leader, with the congregation repeating one of the chosen verses. Or the psalms can be read in alternating couplets by the entire group divided into two parts. A cantor might even chant them in the same manner as the Hebrew psalms.

No matter how they are used, the key is to pray these psalms in a spirit of gratitude and openness to God's word.

B*eatitudes (Luke)*

Luke emphasizes the blessings of those who are not attached to material possessions.

 God, help me to own that the poor are blessed;
the kingdom of heaven is theirs.[1]

Sustain those who are hungry today
by my sharing when I have more than I need.[2]

You bless me in my weeping and in my mourning.
You can turn my tears into laughter.[3]

And blessed am I if I am persecuted,
defamed on account of Jesus.[4]

Gladden my heart that I may rejoice.
My reward is great in heaven.[5]

Empty my life, God, of superfluous wealth.
I await your own consolation.[6]

Temper my greed – my desire for more.
Remind me that some have nothing.[7]

And gentle my laughing – my self-centred fun,
mindful of those who weep.[8]

Let me never depend on human appraisal.
It is you, God, who searches the heart.[9]

Make me loving, forgiving and generous.
I want to be Jesus' disciple.[10]

References

(1)	Lk 6:20	(2)	Lk 6:21
(3)	Lk 6:21	(4)	Lk 6:22
(5)	Lk 6:23	(6)	Lk 6:24
(7)	Lk 6:25	(8)	Lk 6:25
(9)	Lk 6:26	(10)	Lk 6:27-31

*B*eatitudes *(Matthew)*

Matthew emphasizes the blessings of those who recognize their need for God, and who, like God, live lovingly.

 'Draw me, God, into poorness of spirit
as I journey to the heavenly kingdom.'[1]

Make holy my mourning for those in distress.
May I taste your Spirit's comforting.[2]

In gentleness, let me open my heart
to whatever your goodness has planned.[3]

As I hunger and thirst for a world that is just,
give me the fullness Christ promised.[4]

In mercy and outgoing kindness of heart,
I too will receive your mercy.[5]

Cleanse my heart from all ungodliness
so that I may see you, my God.[6]

As a bearer of peace, embracing all,
your very own child shall I be.[7]

And when faith brings me suffering for right,
I know it is the road to the kingdom.[8]

In times of trial, when falsely accused,
fill me with joy and gladness.[9]

Like the prophets before me, I cling to your promise
– fullness of joy in your presence.[10]

References

(1)	Mt 5:3	(2)	Mt 5:4
(3)	Mt 5:5	(4)	Mt 5:6
(5)	Mt 5:7	(6)	Mt 5:8
(7)	Mt 5:9	(8)	Mt 5:10
(9)	Mt 5:11	(10)	Mt 5:12

Blessing

God always blesses his people with love and deeds. Our response is to bless or praise God for this and bless others with the blessings received.

'Blessed be the God and Father of our Lord Jesus
      Christ,
who has blessed us in Christ with every spiritual
      blessing
in the heavenly places.'[1]

Blessed be the God of mercies, the God of all
      consolation.
In all my afflictions, I am consoled.
May I share this blessing with others.[2]

With a grateful heart let me sing psalms and hymns
and spiritual songs to my God,
for within me is dwelling the word of Christ.
May I know its richness in depth.[3]

Mold my heart into love for my enemies,
give those who wish me ill a blessing.
Bring me to offer goodness for hate
and to pray for those who mistreat me.[4]

You blessed us in the bread you broke
and in the wine you poured.
Transform me God into blessing.[5 & 6]

God, you give me every blessing in abundance.
There is always enough of everything.
Take all reluctance out of my life.
Make me cheerful in giving.[6]

≈

Give me the faith of Abraham, who believed
and went forth without knowing.
Gift me with the blessing of those who believe.
Bless all families of the earth.[7]

≈

Worthy is the Lamb that was slain
to receive power and wealth,
wisdom and might and honor,
glory and blessing forever.[8]

≈

Let me never exchange the truth for a lie
by worshipping and serving created things;
but strengthen my faithfulness to you, my creator,
who is blessed forever. Amen.[9]

References

(1) Eph 1:3   (2) 2 Cor 1:3, 4
(3) Col 3:16   (4) Lk 6:27, 28
(5) 1 Cor 10:16   (6) 2 Cor 9:7, 8
(7) Heb 11:8, 9   (8) Rev 5:11-13
(9) Rom 1:25

B^{ody}

Because God became human, all creation is forever blessed. Our bodies are especially blessed because the Holy Spirit lives in us.

 'And the word became flesh and lived among us.'[1]

In Christ dwells bodily the whole fullness of deity.[2]

I know, God, that within me your own spirit dwells.
Your temple is holy and I am that temple.[3]

I am not my own; I have been bought at a price.
Yours is the gift I carry; I glorify you in my body.[4]

Let not sin dominate my body
making it an instrument of wickedness.
Instead may I present my body to you
as an instrument of righteousness.[5]

Worry not about food and clothing;
of more worth my life, my body.
You know, God, that I need these things.
Deepen my trust in you.[6]

Keep blameless my spirit, soul and body
at the coming of Jesus Christ.
He is the one who calls – the faithful one.
You will do this for me.[7]

I am approaching the sanctuary, my body,
with a true heart and faith,
sprinkled clean from an evil conscience,
my body washed in water pure.[8]

~

Fill me with longing for the resurrection of the
  dead,
when what is sown in weakness is raised in power.
Then imperishability and immortality will be
  mine.[9]

~

Now, as always, whether by life or death,
may Christ be exalted in my body.[10]

References

(1)	Jn 1:14	(2)	Col 2:9
(3)	1 Cor 3:16, 17	(4)	1 Cor 6:19, 20
(5)	Rom 6:12, 13	(6)	Lk 12:22-31
(7)	1 Thess 5:23	(8)	Heb 10:22
(9)	1 Cor 15:42-54	(10)	Phil 1:20

*C*elebration

Celebration is the first and deepest response to the feeling of being loved.

 I rejoice in my God always
and again I will rejoice.
May my gentleness be known to everyone,
for God is near.[1]

I will rejoice ever and always;
unceasing be my prayer,[2]
asking and receiving,
completing my joy.[3]

I will work for joy with others,
standing firmly in the faith,[4]
rejoicing even when hated.
In heaven my reward is great.[5]

I rejoice in the truth for such is love,[6]
suffering patiently, faithful in prayer,
in hope rejoicing with all.[7]

In the spirit of God, I rejoice,
celebrating with thanksgiving,
for as God's little one
I have been shown the mysteries of the kingdom.[8]

I will rejoice and be glad in Jesus
for the Father is greater than he
and his Spirit the Advocate he has sent.[9]

PRAYING THE NEW TESTAMENT AS PSALMS

With me he has shared all this
that I may know his joy,
a joy unbounded – complete.[10]

References

(1)	Phil 4:4	(2)	1 Thess 5:16, 17
(3)	Jn 16:24	(4)	2 Cor 1:24
(5)	Lk 6:22, 23	(6)	1 Cor 13:6
(7)	Rom 12:12, 14	(8)	Lk 10:21
(9)	Jn 14:28 & 16:5-7	(10)	Jn 15:11

*C*hrist — *Authority*

Christ's authority is his authorization by God to help us grow towards being our best selves.

 God, who can resist your will?
Who am I to argue with you?
Will what is molded say to the one who molds:
Why have you made me like this?
Has the potter no right over the clay
to make something for ordinary use, something for
    special?[1]

◈

You have granted your Son to have life in himself
and given him authority to pass judgement
because he is the Son of Man.[2]

◈

For now has come the salvation,
the power and the kingdom that is your own,
the authority of your Messiah.[3]

◈

To Jesus has been given all authority in heaven and
    on earth.[4]
He has authority over all people, all things.[5]

◈

His the authority that offers forgiveness,
that casts demons out,
that teaches as no other has taught,
that passes judgement justly.[6]

◈

As I receive him and believe in his name,
he gives in abundance the gift of life,
the power to become a child of God.[7]

References

(1)	Rom 9:19-21	(2)	Jn 5:26, 27
(3)	Rev 12:10	(4)	Mt 28:18
(5)	Jn 17:2		
(6)	Mk 2:10 & 3:14, 15 & Mt 7:29 & Jn 5:30		
(7)	Jn 1:12 & Jn 10:10		

Christ – Human

God became fully human; he walked the journey of life before us and now he walks that journey with each of us.

 'And the Word became flesh and lived among us.'[1]
God, your Son Jesus emptied himself,
taking the form of a servant,
and was born in human likeness.[2]

Conceived and born of a virgin,
wrapped in bands of cloth,
laid in a manger, no place in the inn,
Christ human, one of us.[3]

Like me in every respect, yet sinless
and tested by what he suffered,
he is my merciful and faithful high priest,
able to atone for all my sins and to help me when I
    too am tested.[4]

Knowing that Jesus can sympathize with my
    weaknesses
and that mercy and grace are there for the asking,
I turn to him in my every need
and come to the throne of grace.[5]

You deal with me gently, Jesus,
with the ignorance and the waywardness that is mine,[6]
and you weep over our sinful world
tears of tenderness and compassion.[7]

You knew tiredness as you sat by the well[8]
and grieved over hardness of heart,[9]
experienced hunger from weeks in the desert[10]
and had nowhere to lay your head.[11]

≈

You joined in the banquet prepared by Levi,[12]
and in Cana's wedding feast.[13]
You loved your visits to Martha and Mary[14]
and children you gently caressed.[15]

≈

Bring me to understand clearly, God,
that all life's moments are sacred,
whether joyous or sad, whether painful or glad,
all are experienced in Jesus.[16]

References

(1) Jn 1:14   (2) Phil 2:5-7
(3) Lk 1:31 & 2:6, 7   (4) Heb 2:16-18
(5) Heb 4:15, 16   (6) Heb 5:2
(7) Lk 19:41   (8) Jn 4:6
(9) Mk 2:5-8   (10) Lk 4:1, 2
(11) Lk 9:58   (12) Lk 5:29
(13) Jn 2:1, 2   (14) Jn 11:5
(15) Mk 9:36   (16) Rom 8:28 & 12:15

*C*hrist – *Icon of God*

Jesus is the full human manifestation of what God is and how God acts. He mediates God to us.

 You are the Word become flesh.
In you I see the glory of the Father's only Son.[1]

In you was life and that life was the light of all people.
The true light that enlightens me
has come into the world.[2]

Sent by God, you spoke the words of God.
You alone have seen the Father,
and to you without measure the Spirit was given.[3]

You are the way, the truth and the life.
Through you, all come to the Father.[4]

Knowing you means knowing the Father,
and seeing you is seeing the Father too.[5]

You spoke as the Father instructed,
knowing that the One who sent you is true.[6]

Your prayer – that all may be one –
enables my belief in the One who sent you.[7]

You said, 'Father, glorify your name.'
In answer to you, a voice came from heaven:
'I have glorified it and I will glorify it again.'[8]

~

The Father dwells in you,
and within the Father you also dwell.[9]

~

You were heard and seen by human eye,
looked at and touched by human hands
– the Word of life revealed to the world –
Christ, icon of God.[10]

References

(1)	Jn 1:14	(2)	Jn 1:4-9
(3)	Jn 3:32-34	(4)	Jn 14:6
(5)	Jn 14:7-9	(6)	Jn 8:28 & 7:28, 29
(7)	Jn 1:7, 21	(8)	Jn 12:27, 28
(9)	Jn 14:9, 10	(10)	1 Jn 1:1-3

Christ – King

God's kingdom exists and grows wherever there is goodness, peace and joy brought by the Holy Spirit and human cooperation. Christ is the kingdom in person.

God, the blessed and only Sovereign,
King of kings and Lord of lords,
alone, immortal, dwelling in light unapproachable.
No one has ever seen you.
No one can behold you.
To you be honour and eternal dominion.[1]

Your Son Jesus, Son of the Most High,
receives the throne of his ancestor David,
reigning over the house of Jacob forever.
His kingdom is unceasing.[2]

Jesus, you called me into your kingdom[3]
– a kingdom not of this world –
a kingdom not from here.[4]

Guide me into sinlessness, Jesus,
that I may inherit the fullness of your kingdom,[5]
where the righteous will shine bright as the sun[6]
when your kingdom comes with power.[7]

Your kingdom, like the mustard seed
sown in the field, becomes like a tree
offering shelter to the birds of the air,
lovingly caressing the nests they prepare.[8]

Your kingdom, like a discovered treasure
hidden for long in a field,
brings such joy to the finder
that all else rates as nothing.[9]

≈

As a disciple entrusted with the mysteries of
    heaven[10]
I long for the invitation of Jesus:
Come and inherit the kingdom of God,
prepared when the world was founded.[11]

References

(1)   1 Tim 6:13-16   (2)   Lk 1:32, 33
(3)   Lk 23:42, 43   (4)   Jn 18:36, 37
(5)   Eph 5:5   (6)   Mt 13:43
(7)   Mk 9:1   (8)   Mt 13:31, 32
(9)   Mt 13:44   (10) Mt 13:10, 11
(11) Mt 25:34

*C*hrist – Liberator

Jesus was totally free from all slavery to sin and selfishness. His Spirit offers us the same freedom.

 God, you alone I worship; you alone I serve.
From thirst for status and greed for possessions free
me.[1]

From violence of all kinds free me, God,
that I may live the gentleness of Jesus.[2]

May my heart be so filled with the spirit of the law
that regard for the person be my first concern.[3]

When rejected because of your message,
free me from dependence on people.[4]

In bodily needs, may I know self-control,
remembering your word is nourishment and life.[5]

Let human respect never deter me
from reaching out to those in need.[6]

God, your giftedness abounds in all creation.
May sexism never mar my giving.[7]

Draw all people into oneness with you
that all may be brother and sister and mother.[8]

PRAYING THE NEW TESTAMENT AS PSALMS

May total acceptance be mine at death
and my hope become resurrection to glory.[9]

References

(1)   Lk 4:5-8   (2)   Mt 26:51, 52, 67
(3)   Mk 2:23-28   (4)   Jn 6:66, 67
(5)   Mt 4:1-4   (6)   Lk 19:5-10
(7)   Jn 4:27   (8)   Mt 12:46-50
(9)   Jn 10:18

*C*hrist – Messiah

The word 'messiah' means 'the anointed one', the 'Christ' chosen and sent by God.

 Christ, the Messiah, has come.
He is the light of all people,
the light that shone in the darkness,
which the darkness did not overcome.[1]

I pray that everyone may believe in his name
and be given the power to become children of
    God.[2]

Let me know in depth, God, all that Christ
    proclaims.
Let me hear his voice: 'I am He.'[3]

Remembering that he is your Word become flesh
living among us, showing your glory
full of grace and truth.[4]

Deepen, God, my belonging to the truth
that I may listen to your voice in Jesus.[5]

He sought not glory for himself;
it was you who glorified him.[6]

May I show by my works that you have sent me.
Deepen my faith in Jesus.[7]

I will make your name known
to all who pass my way.[8]

≈

Keep me faithful to your word
that I may never see death.[9]

≈

I have heard that word.
I believe in the One who sent you.
Thank you for bringing me from death to life,
for giving me the gift of grace and truth.[10]

References

(1) Jn 1:4-13   (2) Jn 1:12
(3) Jn 4:25, 26   (4) Jn 5:24
(5) Jn 18:37   (6) Jn 8:50 & 16:14
(7) Jn 10:37, 38 & 14:11   (8) Jn 17:6
(9) Jn 5:36-38   (10) Jn 1:14

*C*hrist – *Mystery*

The mystery of God and of Christ is something so beautiful and so deep that it is endlessly rich.

 How great the glory of the mystery
that you, God, have chosen to make known
– the mystery that is Christ in us, our hope of
glory.[1]

≈

Help us to proclaim and teach in all wisdom
that all may come to maturity in Christ.[2]

≈

We thank you, God, for the grace you have given
– the news of the boundless riches of Christ.[3]

≈

Let everyone see the plan of the mystery,
hidden for ages with you.[4]

≈

Gift us anew with the wisdom of your Spirit,
who searches even the depths of God.[5]

≈

Strengthen us according to the Gospel of Jesus,
proclaiming the mystery kept secret for long ages.[6]

≈

Without doubt, the mystery of our religion is great.
We are Christ's servants and stewards of your
mysteries.[7]

≈

Open for us a door for the Word
That we may declare the mystery of Christ.[8]

≫

Encourage all hearts and unite us in love,
that we may have the riches of assured
    understanding
and the knowledge of your mystery, Christ
    himself.[9]

≫

With all wisdom and insight, according to your
    good pleasure,
we pray that all things be gathered up in Christ
and live for the praise of his glory.[10]

References

(1)	Col 1:27	(2)	Col 1:28
(3)	Eph 3:3	(4)	Eph 3:9
(5)	1 Cor 2:9-11	(6)	Rom 16:25-27
(7)	1 Tim 3:16 & 1 Cor 4:1	(8)	Col 4:3, 4
(9)	Col 2:2, 3	(10)	Eph 1:7-11

Christ – Obedient

Christ's obedience was a trustful willingness to search for, to listen to and to live out God's loving will for him.

 'See, God, I have come to do your will'
were the words of Christ coming into the world.[1]

Through the offering of the body of Christ for all,
I have now been sanctified.[2]

Jesus, your food was to do your Father's will
– for he sent you to complete his work.[3]

You did nothing on your own
but spoke as God had instructed you.[4]

Like you, may I know that I am never alone
as I strive to do what is pleasing to God.[5]

Help me to glorify God on earth
by finishing the work God gives me to do.[6]

Mold my mind into yours,
you who emptied yourself,
obedient to death.[7]

May I say: 'Not my will but yours be done,'
as you prayed in pain and suffering.[8]

May I lose nothing of all you have given me,
and may I be raised up on the last day.[9]

✿

For this is indeed your will for me,
that I who have seen and believe in you
may have eternal life.[10]

References

(1)   Heb 10:5-10   (2)   Heb 10:10
(3)   Jn 4:34   (4)   Jn 8:28
(5)   Jn 8:29   (6)   Jn 17:4
(7)   Phil 2:5-9   (8)   Lk 22:42
(9)   Jn 6:38-40   (10) Jn 6:40

*C*hrist – Praying

Jesus' entire life was lived in union with his Father, yet often he went apart for special moments of intimacy.

 God, your Son Jesus, knowing it was time to
    choose his apostles
spent time in prayer out in the hills
– even whole nights in prayer.[1]

The word about him spread;
the people gathered to hear him,
the crowds clamoured for healing,
but he withdrew alone to pray.[2]

I ask that you teach me to pray,
just as Jesus taught his disciples.
May 'Abba, Father' always be my prayer,
prayer in faith – expectant.[3]

I too pray for the unity for which Jesus prayed
that all people may be one.[4]

May I persevere in asking,
always remembering my need to pray with hope.[5]

May your own spirit descend upon me[6]
as I pray in union with Jesus,
praying that trials may never overpower me,
that you keep me always in faith.[7]

In times of pain and suffering
let my posture of heart be like that of Jesus:
'Father, if you are willing, remove this cup from
    me;
yet, not my will but yours be done.'[8]

≈

You will protect us all in your name our God
– such was the prayer of Jesus,[9]
as we grow more and more into him
until all are as one.[10]

References

(1)	Lk 6:11, 12	(2)	Lk 5:15, 16
(3)	Lk 11:1-4	(4)	Jn 17:11
(5)	Lk 11:5, 8	(6)	Lk 3:21, 22
(7)	Lk 22:31, 32	(8)	Lk 22:41, 42
(9)	Jn 17:15	(10)	Jn 17:21-23

Christ – God's Word

In reply to Moses' question 'Who are you?', God said 'I Am'. Jesus uses the same words about his divine identity from all eternity.

In the beginning was the Word
and the Word was with God
and the Word was God.[1]

In truth you could say:

Through the Word all things came into being.
Without the Word nothing had life.[2]

All things are sustained by this powerful Word[3]
– the Word seated at God's right hand.

You are the Word, the radiance of God's own glory,
the image of the invisible God,
the first-born of all creation.
In you were created all things in heaven and on
earth.[4]

You yourself are before all things
and in you all things hold together.
The fullness of God was pleased to dwell in you.[5]

In truth you could say:
'Before Abraham was, *I Am*.'[6]

You proclaimed what you had seen and heard,
you, the one who comes from heaven.[7]

❧

Though you were in the form of God
You did not exploit the equality.
You emptied youself and became as a servant,
obedient to death on a cross.[8]

❧

So let every creature in heaven and on earth,
and all that is in the sea,
give blessing, honour, glory and might
to the Lamb who was slain.[9]

References

(1) Jn 1:1   (2) Jn 1:2, 3
(3) Heb 1:3, 4   (4) Col 1:15, 16
(5) Col 1:17-19   (6) Jn 8:58
(7) Jn 3:31, 32   (8) Phil 2:6-8
(9) Rev 5:11-14

Christ – Shepherd

Shepherd is the metaphor frequently used in scripture to describe God's loving guidance and care for us.

 In the past, God, you called yourself 'Shepherd of
        Israel,'
and your Son Jesus is our good shepherd.[1]

As the sheep know the voice of their shepherd,
may I know your voice in the midst of life's
        turmoil.[2]

Like Jesus, may I always be among your own,
encountering you ever more deeply.[3]

Look on your people when harassed and helpless,
like sheep without a shepherd.[4]

Help me to extend a welcome to all
– 'one flock, one shepherd' – Christ's prayer.[5]

Increase the Jesus life in me
– life in abundance, life to the full.[6]

In my shepherding, may I be prepared
to lay down my life for others.[7]

Bring me to see my need to believe,
as the shepherds knew their need.
They were the first to hear the good news
– the news of Jesus' birth.[8]

≈

May I be an example to others,
as we journey in faith together,
and you, the chief shepherd, will give me the
    crown,
the crown of unfading glory.[9]

References

(1) Jn 10:11
(2) Jn 10:4
(3) Jn 10:14, 15
(4) Mt 9:36
(5) Jn 10:16
(6) Jn 10:10
(7) Jn 10:11
(8) Lk 2:8-20
(9) 1 Pet 5:3, 4

*C*hrist – *Suffering*

*Authentic love is always expressed in a willingness to suffer for the well-being
and happiness of the loved one.*

 'My Father, if it is possible let this cup pass from me;
yet not what I want but what you want.'[1]

For his was the blood of the covenant
poured out for many for the forgiveness of sins.[2]

I pray, God, for courage in my own times of
    suffering.
My spirit is indeed willing, but my flesh is weak.[3]

Give me the wisdom to know when to speak
and the Christ-likeness that enables silence.[4]

In desolate moments, let me join in Jesus' prayer:
'My God, my God, why have you forsaken me?'[5]

Move deeply my heart, God, as I ponder Christ's
    passion,
like the whole of creation that quaked in shock.[6]

Let me never, like Pilate, wash away my fear of
    suffering with Jesus
in the pain of those around me.[7]

Like the women on Calvary, true to the end,
may no suffering weaken my discipleship.[8]

≋

I remember the promise of Christ's resurrection
that one day I will be raised immortal.[9]

Reference

(1)	Mt 26:39	(2)	Mt 26:28
(3)	Mt 26:41	(4)	Mt 27:14
(5)	Mt 27:46	(6)	Mt 27:51-53
(7)	Mt 27:24	(8)	Mt 27:56
(9)	Mt 20:19		

*C*ompassion

The central theme of the New Testament is God's compassion for us – a compassion that we are privileged to share with one another.

 God, as one of your chosen, holy and beloved,
clothe me with compassion and kindness.[1]

Like Jesus, may I be moved with compassion
as I reach out to others with healing.[2]

God, you are compassionate and merciful.
Make me your mercy, your compassion.[3]

Let me be a shepherd to others,
ready to speak with compassion.[4]

By your loving mercy, your tender compassion,
the dawn from on high has broken upon me.[5]

'Do not weep' were Jesus' own words of
    compassion
to the widow, bereft and grieving.[6]

And the leprous body drew forth deep compassion:
'I do choose' said Jesus and healed him.[7]

With sympathy, love and unity of spirit,
may tenderness dwell in my heart.[8]

I long to experience the compassion of Christ more
    deeply.
God, fulfil my longing.[9]

≈

Give me a heart that is gentle and humble
merging evermore into Jesus.[10]

References

(1)	Col 3:12	(2)	Mk 1:41
(3)	Jas 5:11	(4)	Mk 6:34
(5)	Lk 1:76-78	(6)	Lk 7:13
(7)	Mk 1:41	(8)	1 Pet 3:8
(9)	Phil 1:8	(10)	Mt 11:29

Conscience

Conscience is all of the human person at one's most centered, most free and most responsible moments of choice.

  With a clear conscience,
let me hold to the mystery of faith,
thanking God as our ancestors did.[1]

In everything, let me aim for a clear conscience,
clear before God and all,
for God sees me for what I am.
May my conscience do so too.[2]

When asked the reason for our hope,
let me have my answer ready,
given with courtesy, conscience clear,
showing respect for all.[3]

Faith, God, and a good conscience are my weapons.
May my faith not be shipwrecked
by ignoring my conscience.[4]

True, my conscience may not reproach me,
but that does not mean justification.
God is my judge.[5]

Let me then be obedient,
not only because of retribution,
but also for conscience's sake.[6]

In truth, not pretence,
let me always speak in Christ,
with my conscience testifying for me
in the Holy Spirit.[7]

References

(1) 1 Tim 3:9 & 2 Tim 1:3   (2) Acts 24:16 & 2 Cor 5:11
(3) 1 Pet 3:15   (4) 1 Tim 1:19
(5) 1 Cor 4:4   (6) Rom 13:5
(7) Rom 9:1

_C_ ovenant

The Covenant is the expression of God's unconditional love and fidelity to us;
it is a promise that will never be broken.

 God, you are blessed forever and ever.
You chose a people to be your own.[1]

To them, the covenant and the promises belong,
and from their patriarchs, according to the flesh,
the Messiah, Jesus, came.[2]

In Jesus, we who once were far off
have been brought near by the blood of Christ.[3]

The promises were made to Abraham and his
    offspring,
that is to one person who is Christ.[4]

I thank you, Jesus, for the covenant of your blood
poured out for me and for many.[5]

I pray that, like you, I may become a 'yes'
– 'yes' to every one of God's promises.[6]

Through you, the mediator of the new covenant,
I can receive the promised inheritance.[7]

Deepen in me, God, the Spirit of covenant,
giving life to my ministry with others.[8]

I thank you for looking on me with favour
and redeeming me through Jesus, a mighty saviour.[9]

～

Remembering your covenant with me always,
may I serve you in holiness all my days.[10]

References

(1)	Eph 1:3, 4	(2)	Rom 9:4, 5
(3)	Eph 2:13	(4)	Gal 3:16
(5)	Mk 14:24	(6)	2 Cor 1:19, 20
(7)	Heb 9:15	(8)	2 Cor 3:4-6
(9)	Lk 1:68, 69	(10)	Lk 1:70-74

Co-Workers with God

By our prayer and by our loving actions, God continues to work through us bringing to others the Good News that they are loved.

 God, you are rich in mercy and loved us even as
    sinners.
You made us alive together with Christ.
Your grace has saved us.[1]

Help me declare what I have seen and heard.
Then fellowship is shared
and my joy complete.[2]

I pray that my sharing of faith be effective
as I see all the good I can do for Christ.[3]

My goal is to be with you, God, forever.
With these words, let me encourage everyone.[4]

I share in the grace of God with others.
May we hold one another in our hearts.[5]

In our giving and receiving, may we all be free
– always in the spirit of the Gospel.[6]

May we devote ourselves to the message of Jesus
and grow more truly in fellowship.[7]

I want to know Christ and the power of his rising,
sharing his sufferings – like him in his death.[8]

If I am a child of God, I am also an heir
– heir of God with others
and joint heirs with Christ.[9]

Let me be a partner and co-worker in service,
sharing God's grace in fellowship.[10]

References

(1) Eph 2:4, 5
(2) 1 Jn 1:3, 4
(3) Philem v. 6
(4) 1 Thess 4:17, 18
(5) Phil 1:7
(6) Phil 4:15
(7) Acts 2:42
(8) Phil 3:10
(9) Rom 8:17
(10) 2 Cor 8:23

Death

Believers share with others the sad partings of death. For them, however, it is not the end but resurrection into a new and eternal life.

 Praised be God the Father of our Lord Jesus Christ,
who, in his great mercy, has given me a new birth
into a living hope through the resurrection of Jesus
    Christ from the dead.[1]

One day my mortal nature will become immortal,
and my glorified body will reflect my glorified life
    with Christ.[2]

Though willing to stay alive and share the Good
    News,
deepen my desire to be with Christ.[3]

By my life or by my death,
may Christ be exalted now and always in my body.[4]

As I come to the end of my journey
– a life lived in love for others –
may I breathe Jesus' final words: 'It is fulfilled.'[5]

When my life on earth is ending and my time has
    come to depart,
may I know that I have fought the good fight to
    the end,
that I have run the race to the finish,
and that I have kept the faith.[6]

Then there will be a crown of righteousness
that the upright judge will give to me on that day,
not only to me but to all those who long for his
   appearing.[7]

🙾

I know that when my earthly tent is folding up,
there is a house for me from God,
not made by human hands
but everlasting in the heavens.[8]

🙾

My faith, more valuable than gold, will have been
   tested by all sorts of trials,
and so I will be certain of its goal – the salvation of
   my soul.[9]

🙾

Surely, then, my friends need not grieve without
   hope,
for just as God has brought Jesus to life again,
in the same way he will bring me
and all who believe in his name.[10]

References

(1)	1 Pet 1:3	(2)	1 Cor 15:39-54
(3)	Phil 1:23	(4)	Phil 1:20
(5)	Jn 19:30	(6)	2 Tim 4:6-7
(7)	2 Tim 4:8	(8)	2 Cor 5:1
(9)	1 Pet 1:6-9	(10)	1 Thess 4:13, 14

Detachment

Life is a journey towards freedom and away from enslaving attachments that shackle us.

 As the wheat grain falls into the ground and dies,
it bears abundant fruit.
May I die to selfish life in this world,
always remembering life eternal.[1]

Make me strong, God, with the strength of your
power
against the spiritual forces of evil.[2]

In discipline, in alertness and in self-control
let me resist, steadfast in faith.[3]

My old corrupt self has been put away.
In your likeness, God, renew me.[4]

Gift me with contentment of heart
– contentment with what I have.[5]

Like the poor widow who gave her very last coin,
mold me into total giving.[6]

Though life be fading, may I never lose heart.
My inner nature is renewed day by day.[7]

Since all is your gift, God,
let us hold things in common,
sharing with all those in need.[8]

≈

Detach me from the love of possessions and wealth.
Let me follow your Son without grieving.[9]

≈

Bring me to see everything as loss for Christ,
that I may be found in him.[10]

References

(1)	Jn 12:24-26	(2)	Eph 6:10-17
(3)	1 Cor 9:24-27 & 1 Pet 5:9	(4)	Eph 4:22-24
(5)	1 Tim 6:6-10	(6)	Lk 21:1-4
(7)	2 Cor 4:16-18	(8)	Acts 2:44, 45
(9)	Mt 19:16-22 & Lk 21:1-4		
(10)	Phil 3:7-9		

Discernment

Discernment is a striving to discover God's will. It is a continuous search for the paths that lead to our true happiness.

God, I am from you.
I believe your words.
Give me an open mind and heart
to hear and discern more deeply.[1]

Though I have never heard your voice nor seen
     your form,
let your word abide in me.
I believe in the One you sent.[2]

So keep all foolishness from my life
and lead me in understanding your will.[3]

Fill me with the knowledge of your will
in all spiritual wisdom and understanding.
Then my life can be worthy of you,
bearing fruit in every good work.[4]

Transform me, God, by renewing my mind
that I may discern your will,
trying to discover what is pleasing to you,
what is good, acceptable and perfect.[5 & 6]

Release in me the gifts of your spirit
that I may discern all things.
Praying for others, and they for me,
may we come to maturity
and assurance in all that you will.[7 & 8]

≈

May you, the God of peace,
who brought Jesus back from the dead,
make me complete in everything good,
in all that is pleasing in your sight.[9]

References

(1)	Jn 8:47	(2)	Jn 5:37, 38
(3)	Eph 5:17	(4)	Col 1:9, 10
(5)	Rom 12:2	(6)	Eph 5:10-17
(7)	1 Cor 2:14, 15	(8)	Col 4:12
(9)	Heb 13:20, 21		

*D*iscipleship

Discipleship is our dedication to Christ and our decision to allow him to live again in us.

 Divest me, God, of unnecessary possessions,
that I may be a true disciple.[1]

Teach me to pray 'Abba, Father'
as Jesus taught his disciples.[2]

You send me to proclaim your kingdom
and you empower me with your healing.[3]

Detach me even from family
and from life itself
– freedom for total discipleship.[4]

Let me be a servant to others,
remembering the example of Jesus,[5]
living his new commandment of love –
the true mark of his disciple.[6]

Make me continue in the word of Jesus,
then I am a disciple indeed.[7]

Open my heart to learn from your Son
– the humble, gentle Jesus.
His yoke is easy and his burden light.
I will find rest for my soul.[8]

May I cling to the way I have learned from Christ,
avoiding all that is evil.[9]

≈

I remember that Jesus is with us always
yes, to the end of time.[10]

References

(1)	Lk 14:33	(2)	Lk 11:1
(3)	Lk 9:1, 2	(4)	Lk 14:33
(5)	Jn 13:13, 14	(6)	Jn 13:34, 35
(7)	Jn 8:31, 32	(8)	Mt 11:28-30
(9)	2 Tim 3:13-15	(10)	Mt 28:20

E*cology*

God made our beautiful world for safe, shared enjoyment. It is our privilege and responsibility to treasure and preserve it.

 God, like Jesus your Son – son of the soil –
merge me into oneness with nature.[1]

Like the lilies of the field and the birds of the air,
free me from undue anxiety.[2]

Make me more truly the salt of the earth,
cherishing each part of creation.[3]

Temper all greed when digging the earth,
reminding us that all is sacred.[4]

Build up my faith in times of terror;
let me hear your 'Peace, be still'.[5]

Help me respect even the ground I tread
– in agony, a rock of support.[6]

May I be a leaven in the midst of our world,
diffusing appreciation and reverence.[7]

May contentment be mine in little things
– a manger, a mustard seed, a loaf.[8, 9 & 10]

Make my heart grateful for the sun and the rains
given to all out of love.[11]

≈

Help me keep pure the environment I enjoy;
we punish ourselves in destroying.[12]

≈

As the sun's light failed at the death of Jesus,
may the earth too mourn my passing.[13]

≈

Let me wait for your promise
– a new earth, a new heaven,
and righteousness at home with all.[14]

References

(1) Jn 1:14   (2) Mt 6:28-30
(3) Mt 5:13   (4) Mt 13:44
(5) Mk 4:39, 40   (6) Mt 26:39
(7) Mt 13:33   (8) Lk 2:7
(9) Mk 4:31, 32   (10) Mt 13:32, 33
(11) Mt 5:44, 45   (12) Jn 21:3
(13) Lk 23:44, 45   (14) 2 Pet 3:13

*E*ncouragement

We each need encouragement on our journey. God always encourages us and asks us to do the same for others.

 With encouragement let me share the truth with
others,
dispelling falsehood and error with careful
instruction.[1]

Much joy and encouragement stem from love,
setting at rest the hearts of God's holy people.[2]

Today and every day may I encourage others,
avoiding the enticement of sin and its hardening,[3]
for I have been given a share in Christ.
May I hold my first confidence to the end.[4]

May I always accept the gift of prophecy
as it speaks to me, encourages me and gives
reassurance.[5]

Through encouragement I can give fresh heart,
and perseverance in faith is strengthened.[6]

In all ways, I can offer encouragement
through the written word and the shared
experience,[7]
bringing delight to the hearts of all.[8]

PRAYING THE NEW TESTAMENT AS PSALMS

In hardship, doubt and times of distress,
my encouraging words can lift the spirit,
with affirmation and hospitality
giving strength for the journey.[9]

References

(1)	2 Tim 4:2	(2)	Philem v. 7
(3)	Heb 3:13	(4)	Heb 3:14
(5)	1 Cor 14:3	(6)	Acts 14:22
(7)	Acts 15:30, 31	(8)	Acts 15:31
(9)	Acts 16:40 & 18:27		

E*ndurance*

All loving calls for endurance. Jesus persevered in loving us, and his Spirit
strengthens us to do the same in loving God and one another.

Remembering that not a hair of my head will
    perish,
give me grace, God, to endure.[1]

Direct my heart to your own love
and lead me to the steadfastness of Christ.[2]

Deepen my spirit of prayerfulness,
that I may never lose heart[3]
but endure like the saints who kept your law
and held fast to the faith of Jesus.[4]

Indeed I am blessed in showing endurance.
The crown of life will be mine.[5]

Even endurance in suffering for right
is my call as disciple of Jesus.
He has left me an example that I may follow his
    steps.[6]

Jesus endured for the sake of the chosen
that they may obtain salvation.
If we have endured with Jesus,
with him we shall also reign.[7]

God of steadfastness,
grant me to live in harmony with others,[8]
pursuing righteousness, godliness and faith,
gentleness, love and endurance.[9]

❧

When hated because of your name, God,
strengthen me to endure to the end.[10]

❧

Let the people be aware of my steadfastness,
in affliction – my faith, my endurance.[11]

References

(1) Lk 21:18, 19
(2) 2 Thess 3:5
(3) Lk 18:1
(4) Rev 14:12
(5) Jas 1:12 & 5:11
(6) 1 Pet 2:20, 21
(7) 2 Tim 2:10-12
(8) Rom 15:5, 6
(9) 1 Tim 6:11
(10) Mk 13:13
(11) 2 Thess 1:4

*E*ucharist

Eucharist means thanksgiving. The body of Christ is for our encouragement and sustenance on the journey of life.

Giving thanks, we receive the bread,
blessed, broken, shared.
We take and eat the body of the Lord
given up for us and for all.[1]

Ȿ

We take the cup while giving thanks,
the cup shed for us and for many.
The blood of Jesus we take and drink.
We do so in memory of him.[2]

Ȿ

I thank you, Jesus, for giving us the food
that endures for eternal life.[3]

Ȿ

Jesus, bread of life, I hunger for you.
Quench my thirst too as I reach out in faith.[4]

Ȿ

Our ancestors ate manna in the wilderness and
died,
but we who eat of the bread from heaven will not
die.[5]

Ȿ

Jesus, you are the living bread.
You give your flesh for the life of the world.
Because I eat this bread I will live forever
– the bread of life freely given.[6]

Ȿ

But if I eat and if I drink, I have eternal life
and on the last day I will know resurrection,
for you will raise me up.[7]

❧

Your flesh is true food and your blood is true drink.
Abide in me, Jesus.
May I abide in you.[8]

❧

In coming to you, I will never be hungry.
By believing in you, I will never thirst.[9]
You will not drive away anyone who comes.
You will lose nothing of all God has given you.[10]

References

(1)	Lk 22:19	(2)	Mt 26:27, 28
(3)	Jn 6:27	(4)	Jn 6:35
(5)	Jn 6:49, 50	(6)	Jn 6:51
(7)	Jn 6:54	(8)	Jn 6:55, 56
(9)	Jn 6:35	(10)	Jn 6:37-39

*F*aith

Faith is belief in God's word and this belief leads to trusting fidelity in our relationship with God.

 God, you are faithful – faithful forever.
You cannot deny yourself.[1]

Give me the assurance of things I hope for
and the conviction of things unseen.[2]

In total trust, like that of Abraham,
may I step out in faith – unknowing.[3]

Deepen my faith in Jesus, your Son,
and eternal life is mine.[4]

May your word abide in me forever,
believing in the one whom you sent.[5]

For as Jesus died and rose again,
my death becomes resurrection through him.[6]

Like the grass of the field clothed by your hand,
may we of little faith know surrender.[7]

Nourish my belief in scripture, in the word
– the word that Jesus has spoken.[8]

I remember that suffering accompanies faith,
a privilege graciously granted.[9]

❧

God, help me to be faithful even till death.
You will give me the crown of life.[10]

References

(1)	2 Tim 2:13	(2)	Heb 11:1-3
(3)	Heb 11:8	(4)	Jn 3:34-36
(5)	Jn 5:37, 38	(6)	1 Thess 4:14
(7)	Mt 6:30, 31	(8)	Jn 2:22
(9)	Phil 1:29	(10)	Rev 2:10

*F**amily*

Good family relationships have their origin in God and they reflect our relationship with God.

 God, gift all parents with deep and lively faith,
like the faith of our ancestors,
handed on through generations.[1]

May the love of husbands for their own bodies
be the same love with which they cherish their
wives.[2]

May wives love their husbands
and tenderly care for their children
making for all a home of gentleness and warmth.[3]

Strengthen young men, God, in self-control,
enabling moderation in everything.[4]

Keep young women, God, self-controlled and
chaste,
valuing the right behaviour of women before them.[5]

Bless the children within our families
with a spirit of obedience and trust.[6]

May parents instruct, not provoke, their children,
so that during life's journey they never lose heart.[7]

Let all provide for relatives and family members,
for this is our duty in faith.[8]

References

(1) 2 Tim 1:4   (2) Eph 5:25-33
(3) Titus 2:4, 5   (4) Titus 2:6
(5) Titus 2:3-6   (6) Col 3:20
(7) Col 3:21   (8) 1 Tim 5:8

*F*atherhood

The Fatherhood of God gives life and sustains it. This is reflected in the privilege and responsibility of human fatherhood.

God, one and only – our Father,
all things are from you;
for you we exist.[1]

℘

I bow my knee before you,
from whom in heaven and on earth
all fatherhood takes its name.[2]

℘

Help fathers to gift their children
with what is right and good,[3]
and give them the wisdom
to lead their children in working together as one.[4]

℘

In times that call for celebration,
let there be joy in abundance.[5]

℘

When forgiveness is needed
may fathers be generous in giving.[6]

℘

Let them realize the value of discipline,
and guidance in your ways.[7]

℘

As fathers plead a cure for their children,
may you listen to their prayers.[8]

℘

May they never provoke children to resentment
lest they lose heart and become discouraged,[9]
but make homes like Joseph of old
with skill and fatherly care.[10]

You are one God and Father of all,
above all, through all and in all, forever.[11]

References

(1)	1 Cor 8:6	(2)	Eph 3:14, 15
(3)	Lk 11:11-13	(4)	Mt 21:28-31
(5)	Mt 22:1, 2	(6)	Lk 15:11-13
(7)	Heb 12:7	(8)	Lk 8:40-42
(9)	Col 3:21	(10)	Mt 2:19-23.
(11)	Eph 4:4-6		

*F*ellowship

God's fellowship with us is reflected in our friendships and in our support of one another.

 Your divine power, God, has given us all we need
and the promises through which we participate in
   your divine nature.[1]

You are a faithful God, calling us into fellowship
– fellowship with Jesus your Son.[2]

Let me try to find what is pleasing to you,
having no part in unfruitful works of darkness.[3]

I was buried with Christ in baptism
and raised with him through faith –
faith in your power, my God.[4]

Make me walk as a child of the light.
There is no fellowship between light and darkness.[5]

The cup we bless – a sharing in Christ's blood;
the bread we break – a sharing in his body.
One bread; one body –
though many, we are one.[6]

In struggle and love we die together.
In struggle and love we live together.
We carry one another in our hearts.[7]

Help me become all things to all people for the
 sake of the Gospel
and to share in its many blessings.[8]

≈

If I die with Christ, I will live with him.
Let me then be dead to sin
and alive to you in Christ Jesus.[9]

≈

The grace of our Lord Jesus Christ,
the love of God
and the fellowship of the Holy Spirit
be with us all.[10]

References

(1)	2 Pet 1:3, 4	(2)	1 Cor 1:9
(3)	Eph 5:11	(4)	Rom 6:4, 5
(5)	2 Cor 6:14	(6)	1 Cor 10:16, 17
(7)	2 Cor 7:3	(8)	1 Cor 9:22, 23
(9)	Rom 6:8-11	(10)	2 Cor 13:13

*F*orgiveness

God forgives our sins. We have but to confess them, accept forgiveness and forgive others in the same way. We remind ourselves of this each time we say the Lord's Prayer.

 Blessed are you, God, the Father of our Lord Jesus
    Christ,
the God of mercies and of all consolation.[1]

In Jesus I have redemption through his blood
and forgiveness of my sins
through the riches of his grace lavished upon me.[2]

In truth I can say:
where sin increased, grace did all the more abound.[3]

Let me then put away all bitterness and wrath,
all anger, wrangling and slander, malice of every
    kind.[4]

Touch my heart, God, that I may be kind to others,
tender-hearted, ready to forgive
as you in Christ have forgiven me.[5]

May I never repay evil for evil
but sincerely seek to do good,
good to friends and to all.[6]

Let my prayer in union with Jesus ever be:
'Father, forgive them;
they do not know what they are doing.'[7]

❧

For when I stand in prayer,
forgiveness I must give.[8]
Just as I forgive, so am I forgiven.[9]

❧

As your sun, God, shines on the good and the evil
and your rain falls freely on all,
lead me into total loving,
my prayer embracing everyone.[10]

References

(1)	2 Cor 1:3	(2)	Eph 1:7, 8
(3)	Rom 5:20	(4)	Eph 4:31
(5)	Eph 4:32	(6)	1 Thess 5:15
(7)	Lk 23:34	(8)	Mk 11:25
(9)	Mt 6:12-15	(10)	Mt 5:44, 45

*F*reedom

Freedom is a gift from God enabling us to redirect the forces within us that could hinder our human and Christian development.

 'Where the spirit of the Lord is, there is freedom.'
Free me, God, in your spirit.[1]

For I know we are called to freedom,
in loving service to one another.[2]

Christ set me free that I should remain free.
Let me stand firm against loss of freedom.[3]

Even though systems may try to enslave me
I am not a slave to any human master.
Freedom is mine to cherish.
I belong to you, my God.[4]

Many who are slaves of corruption promise
    freedom,
and we are all slave to whatever masters us.
May I never forget that freedom comes
through knowing my Lord and Savior, Jesus
    Christ.[5]

May my liberty not be a stumbling block to
    others,[6]
May I never use my freedom as a pretext for evil.[7]

Bring me more deeply into discipleship.
May I continue in the word of Jesus.
Then I will know the truth,
and the truth will set me free.[8]

≈

I am justified, God, by the gift of your grace
– the grace of freedom in Christ Jesus.[9]

≈

May creation be released from its slavery to
    corruption,
to enjoy this same glorious freedom.[10]

References

(1)	2 Cor 3:17	(2)	Gal 5:13
(3)	Gal 5:1	(4)	1 Cor 7:21, 22
(5)	2 Pet 2:19 20	(6)	1 Cor 8:8, 9
(7)	1 Pet 2:16	(8)	Jn 8:31-36
(9)	Rom 3:24	(10)	Rom 8:21

F riendship

Our friendship with one another is a human manifestation of God's infinite love and friendship for us.

 Thank you, God, for the gift of friendship.
The peacemakers, the friend-makers are blessed.[1]

Lead me to celebrate with others,
rejoicing in mutual love.[2]

Greeting each person by name,
sharing friendship and peace.[3]

In company giving and receiving refreshment,
listening and praying together as one.[4]

When forgiveness is needed, help us, God,
that our friendship may deepen and grow.[5]

Knowing even friends can hurt one another,
make me sincere and open.[6]

Sharing your goodness, God, working within me,
knowing your presence, your love.[7]

With the comforting power of your Spirit, God,
may I comfort all those in need.[8]

In friendship, make genuine my concern for the
    other.
Bring us to caring in depth.[9]

❧

May I pray day and night in my heart
with gratitude for the gift of friends.[10]

References

(1)	Mt 5:9	(2)	Lk 15:6
(3)	Rom 16:1-23	(4)	Rom 15:30, 32
(5)	Mt 26:50	(6)	Lk 22:48
(7)	Mk 5:19	(8)	Col 4:10, 11
(9)	Phil 2:20	(10)	2 Tim 1:3

F*ruit*

An abundance of good fruit grows from healthy roots and branches. By faith we are rooted in God and grafted on to Christ.

Nurture in me, God, the fruit of your Spirit
– love, joy, patience and peace.
Make my heart gentle, generous and kind,
in self-control and faithfulness.[1]

Give me wisdom, pure and from above,
gentle, peaceable, willing to yield.
Then mercy and good works will flow.[2]

We have been given your kingdom, God.
May its fruits show forth in my life.[3]

In ministry, sharing and receiving good fruit
may we always come together as one.[4]

Let me show the peaceful fruit of righteousness
that comes from discipline and pain.[5]

The fruit I bear is the fruit of repentance.
By my fruits let me be known.[6]

I have died to the law through the body of Christ
and now I belong to another
– to Christ, risen from death to life
that together we might bear fruit for God.[7]

When blessed with gifts that are material,
may I seek the spiritual fruits.[8]

≋

United with Christ I bear much fruit;
cut off from him I can do nothing.[9]

≋

May I recognize the false prophets of today;
I will know them by their fruits.[10]

≋

Living in Christ means fruitful labor.
Dying in Christ is gain.
Give me grace, God, to accept life or death
– whatever – in his name.[11]

References

(1) Gal 5:22-23
(2) Jas 3:17
(3) Mt 21:43
(4) Rom 1:11-13
(5) Heb 12:11
(6) Mt 3:7, 8
(7) Rom 7:4
(8) Phil 4:16, 17
(9) Jn 15:5
(10) Mt 7:15-20
(11) Phil 1:22-23

G*lory*

God's glory is the radiant manifestation of his greatness, goodness and beauty.
We share in this glory through Christ living in us.

 I join with the multitude of the heavenly host
        saying:
'Glory to God in the highest.'[1]

To you, God, belong the glory and the power.
Yes, forever and ever.[2]

There is no need of sun or moon in the city of the
        new Jerusalem,
for your glory, God, is its light.
Its lamp is indeed the Lamb.[3]

Jesus is the reflection of your own glory,
the very imprint of your being.[4]

I was buried with him by baptism into death
and raised from the dead by the glory that is yours.[5]

Though I have sinned and fallen short of your
        glory,
I am justified by your gift of grace
through redemption in Christ Jesus.[6]

Like the disciples on Tabor, let me see your glory.
When Christ who is our life is revealed,
I too will be revealed in glory.[7]

≈

Bring me to imperishability, God.
Raise me up in glory.[8]

≈

I ask you to glorify your name in me.
Let me hear your words:
'I have glorified it and will glorify it again.'[9]

≈

God of peace, make me complete in everything
    good,
in all that is pleasing in your sight
through Jesus Christ to whom be the glory
for ever and ever. Amen.[10]

References

(1) Lk 2:13, 14   (2) 1 Pet 4:11
(3) Rev 21:22-26   (4) Heb 1:3
(5) Rom 6:4, 5   (6) Rom 3:23, 24
(7) Lk 9:28-36 & 1 Jn 3:2 (8) 1 Cor 15:42, 43
(9) Jn 12:28   (10) Heb 13:20, 21

God's Love

*God is infinite, unconditional, merciful and faithful love. By the power of
the Holy Spirit, we share in this and mediate it to others.*

God, you loved the world so much
you gave your only Son.
Bring all to faith in Jesus
that eternal life may be theirs.[1]

❧

I want to remain in the love of Jesus.
It was for us that Jesus prayed.[2]

❧

Let us be shepherd one to another,
ready to lay down our lives.[3]
For no one has greater love than this:
to lay down one's life for one's friends.[4]

❧

Your own love, God, has been poured into my
    heart
by the Holy Spirit, which has been given to me.[5]

❧

Jesus, you gave proof of God's love for me.
While I was still a sinner, you died for me.[6]

❧

The fruit of the spirit is love.
Move me into the infinity of your love.[7]

❧

I know that whoever fails to love
does not know the God of love.
You are love itself.
Steep me in your love.[8]

God, you are rich in faithful love
and through that love you raised me in Christ
and gave me a place with him in heaven.[9]

Bring me to know deeply your love
– the love beyond all knowledge.
Fill me with the utter fullness that is yours.[10]

References

(1) Jn 3:16
(2) Jn 15:9 & Jn 17:9
(3) Jn 10:11
(4) Jn 15:12, 13
(5) Rom 5:5
(6) Rom 5:7
(7) Gal 5:22
(8) 1 Jn 4:8-10
(9) Eph 2:4-6
(10) Eph 3:19

God in All

God is the creator from whom all things are and for whom all things exist.
In God we live, move and have our being.

 God, we know that idols are illusions,
that there is no God but you,
you, the one from whom all things come
and for whom we all exist.[1]

How rich and deep are your wisdom and knowledge,
unsearchable your judgements,
inscrutable your ways.[2]

I cannot know your mind, my God.
I can never be your counsellor.
Impossible for me to give you a gift
and receive a gift in return.[3]

You are the blessed and only Sovereign,
the King of kings and Lord of lords.[4]

Alone immortal, dwelling in light, unapproachable.
No one has seen you.
No one can see you.
To you be honor and eternal dominion.[5]

Everything needed for life you have given,
everything pertaining to godliness.[6]

Keep me, God, from the corruption in our world,
forever a participant in your divine nature.[7]

☙

You who made the world and everything in it,
you are not contained in shrines human-made;
you are never far from each one of us.
In you I live, move and have my being.[8]

☙

Let me own your presence in all of creation
– in everything you have made.
To you, my God, whom I know and honor,
I give praise and thanks unceasingly.[9]

☙

For from you, through you and to you are all
    things.
To you be glory forever.[10]

References

(1)	1 Cor 8:4-6	(2)	Rom 11:33
(3)	Rom 11:34, 35	(4)	1 Tim 6:15
(5)	1 Tim 6:16	(6)	2 Pet 1:3
(7)	2 Pet 1:4	(8)	Acts 17:24-28
(9)	Rom 1:18-21	(10)	Rom 11:36

*G*ratitude

After celebration, gratitude is the deepest human response to life and to gifts received.

 Having received Jesus as Lord and Christ,
I live my life in him,
rooted, built up, held firm by faith.
My heart with thanksgiving overflows.[1]

❦

Unworried my life as I gratefully share with God
my desires, my needs.
And a peace unspeakable, the peace of God,
guards my thoughts in Christ.[2]

❦

God, all your creation is good – no food to be
rejected,
made holy by your word and prayer.
May all be received with thanksgiving.[3]

❦

I thank you for the faith of others
– my encouragement in times of distress.[4]

❦

I thank you too for the generosity of friends
– may my gratitude to you overflow.[5]

❦

In Jesus I have been given your grace,
which draws me to constant thanksgiving.[6]

❦

For the gift of spiritual knowledge
may I always be grateful.[7]

~

Let me then sing psalms and hymns and inspired
    songs,
singing and chanting to God in my heart,
giving thanks to the Father through Jesus.[8]

~

In Christ you lead me in triumph,
as, through me, the fragrance of knowing you is
    spread.
I thank you, God.[9]

~

Blessing and glory, wisdom and thanksgiving,
honor and power and might
be to you, our God, for ever and ever. Amen.[10]

References

(1) Col 2:6, 7   (2) Phil 4:6, 7
(3) 1 Tim 4:4, 5   (4) 1 Thess 3:7-9
(5) 2 Cor 9:10-12   (6) 1 Cor 1:4, 5
(7) Lk 17:11-14   (8) Eph 5:19, 20
(9) 2 Cor 2:14   (10) Rev 7:12

*H*ealing

We all need God's constant deep healing and we can minister that healing to one another by prayer, listening, loving deeds and kind words.

 Jesus, you felt the pain of the sick.
You healed them and God was glorified.[1]

❧

Open the door of healing to me.
Only say the word and I will be healed.[2]

❧

You took our infirmities, you have borne our
  diseases
and you still suffer with all who are ill.[3]

❧

You bestowed the gift of healing on your Church.
May this gift ease the brokenness of our human
  lives.[4]

❧

Strengthen my faith; deepen my confession of sin
and increase my spirit of prayer.
Your anointing will bring me healing.[5]

❧

Help me, Jesus, to persevere in prayer
knowing your response will be everything I need.[6]

❧

Guide doctors, nurses and all those who care,
with wisdom in their noble profession.[7]

❧

Remember my friends whose faith and loving
    action
encourage and sustain me in my struggle.
They bring healing in my life.[8]

≫

And give your Church an open ear, a listening heart,
that it may always turn to you and be healed.[9]

≫

When earthly healing may not be mine
and I cry – 'My God, my God, why have you
    forsaken me?'
may I pray – 'Father, into your hands I commend
    my spirit'
with the living hope that one day I will be with you
    in paradise.[10]

≫

With the confident assurance that I need never be
    afraid
I ask for the greatest healing of all – your peace,
a peace the world can never give.[11]

References

(1)	Mt 15:30, 31	(2)	Lk 11:9-13 & Mt 8:5-8
(3)	Mt 8:16, 17		
(4)	Lk 9:1, 2 & Acts 5:15, 16 & 1 Cor 12:9, 28		
(5)	Jas 5:13-16	(6)	Lk 11:5-8
(7)	Mk 5:25, 26	(8)	Mt 9:1-8
(9)	Mt 13:13-18		
(10)	Mt 27:46 & Lk 24:43, 46 & 1 Pet 1:3		
(11)	Jn 14:1, 27		

H*eart*

In scripture, the heart represents the whole person at one's deepest centre.

 God, you know everyone's heart –
our feelings, passions, desires.[1]

You are the searcher of mind and heart.
Release your Spirit still more within me.[2]

Let not hardness seep into my heart.
Your kindness can lead to repentance.[3]

Keep me faithful with heartfelt devotion,
full of the Holy Spirit and faith.[4]

I rejoice that your love is poured into my heart
by your own free gift of the Spirit.[5]

May Christ dwell in my heart through faith,
grounding and rooting me in love.[6]

On my heart, God, your covenant is written:
you are our God; we are your people.[7]

As the morning star rises in my heart,
open me still more to your message.[8]

With humble mind and heart that is tender,
bring me to sympathy and love for all.[9]

∽

And as we grow into unity of spirit
let us refresh each other's hearts in Christ.[10]

References

(1)	Acts 1:24	(2)	Rom 8:27
(3)	Mk 10:6 & Rom 2:4	(4)	Acts 11:23, 24
(5)	Rom 5:5	(6)	Eph 3:17
(7)	Heb 8:10	(8)	2 Pet 1:19
(9)	1 Pet 3:8	(10)	Philem v. 20

*H*oliness

God's holiness is unlimited moral perfection. All are called towards this holiness. In Baptism, we receive the grace to grow in the likeness of God.

'Holy, holy, holy,
the Lord God the almighty,
who was and is and is to come.'[1]

I pray with Jesus
that your name be held holy.[2]

I want to be holy.
You have called me to this.[3]
You are the one who sanctifies.[4]

I thank you for making us a holy nation
– yes, your very own people.[5]

Your grace is able to build me up
and to give me the inheritance
among all who are sanctified.[6]

I have been chosen as the first fruits for salvation
and through belief in the truth
I am sanctified by the Spirit.[7]

Strengthen my heart in holiness, God,
that I may be blameless at the coming of Jesus.[8]

In accordance with your will,
Jesus offered his body once and for all,
enabling my pathway to holiness.[9]

≈

May I present my body to you, our God,
as a living sacrifice, acceptable and holy.[10]

≈

I remember that I was washed and sanctified,
justified in the name of Jesus your Son,
and in the power of your Spirit.[11]

≈

May I greet others with a holy kiss
as we journey towards holiness together.[12]

References

(1)	Rev 4:8	(2)	Mt 6:9
(3)	1 Pet 1:14-16	(4)	Heb 2:11
(5)	1 Pet 2:9	(6)	Acts 20:32
(7)	2 Thess 2:13	(8)	1 Thess 3:13
(9)	Heb 10:10	(10)	Rom 12:1
(11)	1 Cor 6:11	(12)	1 Cor 16:20

Holy Spirit

The Holy Spirit pours God's love into our hearts, enabling us to transform the world with that love.

 God, send your Spirit still more upon me,
that, as one of your anointed,
I may bring good news to the afflicted.[1]

Send me to proclaim release to the captives,
recovery of sight to the blind,
and to let the oppressed go free.[1]

I want to be your witness.
Deepen in me the power of your Spirit.[2]

Open my heart to the guidance of your Spirit
– openness like that of Simeon,[3]
knowing your Spirit will always teach me what I
    ought to say.[4]

Build up our churches with the gift of peace.
May we all know your Spirit's comforting.[5]

May the Spirit so fill our minds and hearts
that we speak your word with boldness.[6]

Let us know in fullness your Spirit's joy,
even when captive to the Spirit without knowing.[7]

PRAYING THE NEW TESTAMENT AS PSALMS

Send your Holy Spirit anew on the earth,
overshadowing it with your power,
that all may be birthed into holiness
and know they are children of God.[8]

≈

I thank you, God of heaven and earth,
and I rejoice in your Holy Spirit,
because things you have hidden from the wise and
    intelligent
you have revealed to infants like me.[9]

≈

My prayer is that all may receive your Spirit
as you lay your hands gently upon them.[10]

≈

Like Stephen, may we be filled with the Spirit
and gaze on your glory in heaven.[11]

References

(1) Lk 4:18   (2) Acts 1:8
(3) Lk 2:27   (4) Lk 12:12
(5   Acts 9:31   (6) Acts 4:31
(7) Acts 13:52 & 20:22   (8) Lk 1:35
(9) Lk 10:21   (10) Acts 8:15, 17
(11) Acts 7:55

H*ope*

Our hope of resurrection rests on God's promise and on the resurrection of Jesus.

 In hope, we were saved.
As I wait in patience for what I do not see,
grace me God with deeper hope.[1]

Make possible my hoping even against hope,
like Abraham, the father of many nations.[2]

You are the God of hope.
Fill me with hope in abundance
by the power of your Holy Spirit.[3]

In exultant expectation,
let me rejoice in my hope of sharing your glory.[4]

In steadfastness, God, let me hold to your word,
open to the encouragement of the Scriptures in
    hope.[5]

I know that Christ is among us always.
He is our hope of glory.[6]

Purify me, God, in my hoping,
that I may be pure as you are pure.[7]

God of truth, lead me to seize the hope set before me
– a sure and steadfast anchor of my soul.[8]

As a lamp shining in a dark place,
make me attentive to the prophetic message while
    the day dawns
and the morning star rises in our hearts.[9]

Through Jesus and through grace,
may I know eternal comfort and hope
– my heart strengthened in every good work and
    word.[10]

References

(1)   Rom 8:24, 25   (2)   Rom 4:18
(3)   Rom 15:13   (4)   Rom 5:1, 2
(5)   Rom 15:4   (6)   Col 1:26, 27
(7)   1 Jn 3:2, 3   (8)   Heb 6:18-20
(9)   2 Pet 1:19   (10) 2 Thess 2:16, 17

H ospitality

Hospitality as welcoming – especially the stranger – is a central biblical theme.

'I was hungry and you gave me food; I was thirsty
    and you gave me something to drink
Come, you that are blessed by my Father,
inherit the kingdom prepared for you.'[1]

For many will come from the east and the west;
from the north and the south they will come.
They will eat in the kingdom, the kingdom of God
– hospitality unending.[2]

Make my giving generous, God, ready to meet all
    needs,
extending hospitality to enemy, to stranger,
according to the gifts you have given.[3]

Let me be like the Samaritan bandaging wounds,
pouring in oil and wine,[4]
or Zacchaeus descending in haste from the tree
in response to the call of Jesus.[5]

This is my blood, poured out for many,
the blood of the new covenant.
This is my body, take and eat,
may our hospitality be Eucharist.[6]

Let me be one with the crippled, the poor,
the blind, the rejected, the lame –
inviting, celebrating, ministering with all
in mutual love and service.[7]

         ≋

May I remember prisoners and those who are
    tortured,
as though I too were unfree,
walking with them and bearing their pain
– one body in Christ are we.[8]

         ≋

May I serve others as a steward of grace,
enabling constant love
– love that covers many a sin, hospitality
    uncomplaining.[9]

         ≋

Like the disciples, I invite Christ to stay,
for the day is now nearly spent.
Renew my faith, Jesus,
make holy our welcoming.
Blessed by your Father am I.[10]

References

(1)	Mt 25:34, 35	(2)	Lk 13:29
(3)	Rom 12:6-20	(4)	Lk 10:29-37
(5)	Lk 19:6	(6)	Mk 14:22-25
(7)	Lk 14:16-21	(8)	Heb 13:1-3
(9)	1 Pet 4:8-10	(10)	Lk 24:28-32

*I*mmortality

Faith in the resurrection of Jesus gives us assurance of immortality in heaven.

God, you are rich in mercy.
You loved me totally, even when dead through my sins,
and brought me to life together with Christ.
By grace I have been saved.[1]

If my hope in Christ were for this life only,
most pitiable indeed would I be,
but as all people died in Adam
so all will be made alive in Christ.[2]

Jesus is the resurrection and the life
and all who live and believe in him will never die.[3]

For my perishable body will put on imperishability,
and my mortal body will be clothed in immortality.
Death will be swallowed up in victory.[4]

Dwelling within me is God's own spirit
giving life to my mortal body
– God, who raised Jesus from the dead.[5]

Like Paul, I experience the suffering of Christ

– Christ living in me,
living by faith in the Son of God
who loved and gave himself for me.[6]

≈

I long for the appearing of the righteous judge
who will give me the crown of righteousness
and to all who have walked with others in their need
to all who have desired his coming.[7]

References

(1)	Eph 2:4, 5	(2)	1 Cor 15:19-22
(3)	Jn 11:24-26	(4)	1 Cor 15:54, 55
(5)	Rom 8:11	(6)	2 Cor 1:5 & Gal 2:20
(7)	2 Tim 4:8		

*J*ohn the Baptizer

As Christians we are all privileged, like John, to help in preparing people's hearts to receive the Redeemer ever more deeply.

 God, in the wilderness of our world
may our message be:
'Repent, for the kingdom of heaven has come
    near.'[1]

Let my life be in keeping with what I proclaim,
my fruits in keeping with my repentance.[2]

My mission is prophet, messenger and herald,
preparing the way for Jesus.[3]

Sent by you, we witness to the light,
that, through us, all might believe.[4]

Let mine be the voice crying out on the earth:
Here is the lamb of God, who forgives the sin of
    the world.
Make straight the way for him.[5]

Give me the courage the Baptist showed
in upholding goodness and right.[6]

May I be a burning and shining lamp
testifying ever to truth.[7]

As the Spirit descended on Jesus your Son,
I too am baptized in the Spirit.
With John I make my prayer of faith:
This is the Chosen One of God.[8]

⁓

Unworthy am I to loose Jesus' sandal.[9]
I am simply a voice, missioned and sent
to bring the good news of the Kingdom.[10]

References

(1)	Mt 3:2	(2)	Mt 3:8
(3)	Mt 11:10	(4)	Jn 1:6-8
(5)	Jn 1:23, 29	(6)	Mt 14:4-12
(7)	Jn 5:35	(8)	Jn 1:33, 34
(9)	Jn 1:27	(10)	Jn 1:23

*J*oseph

No words of Joseph are recorded, but he stands as a model of quiet faith, of service and fidelity.

 Generations have passed and the time has now come.
Joseph is to be guardian of God's only Son.[1]

Joseph, son of David, do not be afraid.
Mary has conceived by God's Holy Spirit.[2]

In my times of anguish, confusion and doubt,
I relate with the agony in Joseph's own heart.[3]

With love I too grieve with Joseph and Mary –
no room at the inn, only a stable.[4]

Let me haste with the shepherds and ponder anew
Mary and Joseph, the child Jesus too.[5]

God is with us – Emmanuel.
The words of the prophet are now fulfilled.[6]

A pair of turtle doves, the gift of the poor.
Yet the name of Jesus means Savior of all.[7]

With authority invested in him and true to the
    angel's word,
Joseph and Mary proclaimed the child's name:
– Jesus, Savior of the world.[8]

I pray for the trust and detachment of Joseph
trudging at night into Egypt,
and, when danger had ceased and the order was
    given,
returning with Mary and Jesus.[9]

≈

Joseph the righteous, guardian of Jesus,
his teacher, confidante and friend,
be with me as I walk the journey of life
and lead me, in faith, to the end.[10]

References

(1)	Mt 1:16, 17	(2)	Mt 1:18-22
(3)	Mt 1:19, 20	(4)	Lk 2:4-7
(5)	Lk 2:15, 16	(6)	Mt 1:22, 23
(7)	Lk 2:22-24	(8)	Lk 2:21
(9)	Mt 2:13-15, 19-23	(10)	Mt 1:14, 21

Journey of Life

At its deepest level, life is a journey with God to God.

God, as Jesus your Son came into the world,
I too experience life's journeying.
May I be ready at journey's end
to leave the world and go to you.[1]

You are the one who sent your Son
and left him not alone.
You are with me because you sent me.
Let me walk with you on my journey.[2]

May I have the confidence, the trust of Jesus,
thanking you, God, for hearing me.
I know that you always hear me.[3]

In love, God, show me all that you are doing.
As I journey, show me even greater things.
I wonder at your power.[4]

I wish to know you as Jesus does,
for I am from you too
and you have sent me.[5]

I have made your name known to many
and will continue to make you known,
so that the love with which you love me may be in
them.[6]

When I meet the cup of suffering
– and from me it cannot pass –
let me embrace it with open hands.
Your will be done, my God.[7]

~

Make me one with your command,
that the world may know my love for you,
for to glorify myself means nothing.
It is you who will glorify me.[8]

~

With Jesus I desire to be with you,
for you loved me before the foundation of the world.
Show me your glory one day.[9]

References

(1)	Jn 16:28	(2)	Jn 8:29
(3)	Jn 11:42, 43	(4)	Jn 5:20
(5)	Jn 7:29	(6)	Jn 17:25, 26
(7)	Mt 26:42	(8)	Jn 14:31
(9)	Jn 8:54	(10)	Jn 17:24

J*oy*

As our faith deepens, so does our joy, even in the midst of life's adversities. Joy is the fruit of the Holy Spirit.

 'My soul magnifies the Lord
and my spirit rejoices in God my Savior.'[1]

The word leaps joyfully in the depths of my being
at the sound of your voice.[2]

Good news and great joy for all people
– a Savior, the Messiah is ours.
I will never be afraid.[3]

Overwhelmed with joy is my heart
at the star brilliantly settled – its journey done.[4]

Though not seeing, I love,
though unbeholding, I believe,
and a joy indescribable and glorious
wells forth in my heart
– the outcome of my faith, the salvation of my
   soul.[5]

Spirit of God, strengthen in me your fruit
– love, peace and joy.[6]

Rising above opposition,
lead me into godliness
joyfully open to your word of life.[7]

For the kingdom is not food and drink
but righteousness, peace and joy in you.[8]

May the God of hope fill me with all joy and peace
    in believing,
and by the power of his Spirit may my heart
    abound in hope.[9]

References

(1)   Lk 1:46, 47   (2)   Lk 1:43, 44
(3)   Lk 2:10, 11   (4)   Mt 2:10
(5)   1 Pet 1:8-9   (6)   Gal 5:22
(7)   1 Thess 1:6   (8)   Rom 14:17
(9)   Rom 15:13

ingdom

The reign of God is growing as people come together in goodness, peace and joy, by the power of the Holy Spirit.

 God in heaven, may your name be kept holy
as we await the coming of your kingdom.[1]

Detach me from unnecessary things
while sharing with the poor and needy.[2]

It is your pleasure to give us the kingdom.
'Do not be afraid, little flock,' says Jesus.[3]

Like Jesus, let me proclaim the good news of the
   kingdom
– a kingdom that cannot be shaken –
rendering thanks with reverence and awe
by which we make our worship acceptable.[4]

The poor of the world are the heirs of the kingdom,
those rich in faith and love.
Bring me to poorness in spirit, God,
that I may be chosen and blessed.[5]

Righteousness, peace and joy in the Spirit –
these are the signs of the kingdom.[6]

Let me live a life worthy of you, God,
who calls me into your kingdom, your glory.[7]

⁐

Like a little child owning my helplessness
may I trust totally, always eager to receive.[8]

⁐

I thank you, God, for rescuing me from the power
of darkness
and transferring me into the kingdom of your Son,
the beloved,
in whom I am redeemed and forgiven.[9]

References

(1) Mt 6:9, 10   (2) Mt 19:21
(3) Lk 12:32   (4) Mt 4:23 & Heb 12:28
(5) Jas 2:5   (6) Rom 14:17
(7) 2 Thess 1:11   (8) Mt 18:2-4
(9) Col 1:1, 3, 14

*L*eadership

Christian leadership is one form of caring service of others. It is a gift given by the Holy Spirit to promote the growth of those being served.

 'You ought to wash one another's feet.
I have set you an example.'[1]

Help us God, to see leadership as service,
remembering that to be first is also to be servant.[2]

As servants of Christ, leaders are stewards of your
    mysteries.
May they be trustworthy in your sight, my God.[3]

Make them hospitable, lovers of goodness,
prudent, upright and self-controlled.[4]

Give them eagerness in tending your flock,
not lording it over them but being an example.[5]

Commissioned by you, God, they are servants of
    the Church.
Let them make your word known in all its fullness.[6]

May no greater joy be theirs than this:
that all your children are walking in the truth.[7]

As your servants, God, help them to be kindly,
teaching with patience, correcting with gentleness.[8]

❧

Let them know that suffering must be endured
as they carry out their ministry, proclaiming the
    word.[9]

❧

The authority you give is for building up each one.
May they never be ashamed of their trust.[10]

References

(1) Jn 13:12-15   (2) Mt 20:25-28
(3) 1 Cor 4:1, 2   (4) Titus 1:8
(5) 1 Pet 5:1-3   (6) Col 1:24-26
(7) 3 Jn v. 4   (8) 2 Tim 2:24-26
(9) 2 Tim 4:1-5   (10) 2 Cor 10:8

*L*ife

God's deepest desire for us is that we have fullness of life in this world and eternal life in the next.

 God of immortality, dwelling in unapproachable
    light,
to you be honor and eternal dominion.[1]

In your great mercy, you have given us a new birth
    in a living hope
by raising your Son Jesus from the dead.[2]

Jesus, you are the resurrection and the life.
Deepen my faith in you that I may live.[3]

Let me live to you, God.
Let me die to you,
that I may truly belong to you
– God of the living and the dead.[4]

Make me a Gospel person – righteous, faith-filled –
for those who are righteous will live by faith.[5]

Your own Spirit dwells within me
giving life to my mortal body
– the Spirit who raised Jesus from the dead.[6]

Let me take hold of the eternal life to which I am
    called.
Let me witness to this calling in the presence of all.[7]

♺

Set my mind, God, on things that are above,
my life hidden with Christ in you.
He is my life.
With him I will be revealed in glory.[8]

♺

By baptism into Christ,
I was baptized into his death
and by his resurrection into glory.
I can now walk in newness of life.[9]

♺

By his death Christ died to sin
but the life he lives he lives to God.
Let me then be dead to sin
and alive to God, in Jesus.[10]

References

(1)	1 Tim 6:16	(2)	1 Pet 1:3
(3)	Jn 11:25, 26	(4)	Rom 14:7-9
(5)	Rom 1:17	(6)	Rom 8:11
(7)	1 Tim 6:12	(8)	Col 3:2-4
(9)	Rom 6:3, 4	(10)	Rom 6:10-11

*L*ight

Jesus is the light of the world, showing us how to live a life of love as he did, and as he continues to do in and through us.

 Your Son Jesus, God, came into the world
to draw us from darkness into light.[1]

Guide my footsteps, light my way
that darkness may never overtake me.[2]

Strengthen among us our togetherness
walking in Jesus, the Light.[3]
For the people in darkness saw a great light
and the shadow of death transformed.[4]

The eyes of Simeon saw your salvation
– for Israel, glory;
– for the Gentiles, a light.[5]

Jesus' face shone like the sun, his garments dazzling
    white.
May I too often experience the radiance of your
    presence.[6]

I thank you, God, for enabling me to share
in the inheritance of the saints in light,[7]
a light that has made us a holy people,
a royal priesthood, a chosen race.[8]

For once I was darkness, but now in the Lord
I live as a child of light.[9]

≈

You, God, have shone in my heart.
May my light shine forth.
To you be the praise and the glory.[10]

References

(1) Jn 12:46   (2) Jn 12:35, 36
(3) 1 Jn 1:5-7   (4) Mt 4:13-16
(5) Lk 2:30-32   (6) Mt 17:2
(7) Col 1:11-14   (8) 1 Pet 2:9
(9) Eph 5:8   (10) 2 Cor 4:4-6 & Mt 5:14-16

*L*istening

As we develop listening hearts before God's word, we grow in faith and love.

I thank you, God, for the gift of faith
that came to us through hearing Christ's word.[1]

Gift me with a listening heart
and deepen in me the understanding that your
      Spirit gives.[2]

Let me be generous in sharing faith,
telling others what I hear and see.[3]

May hearts that are dull and ears deaf with
      hardening
become open to your healing power.[4]

Keep me always united in faith,
listening and receiving the message of Jesus.[5]

Always aware of your voice from the cloud:
'This is my Son, the Beloved; listen to him!'[6]

I too have received grace and a call
to bring about the obedience of faith in others.[7]

Send forth your Spirit anew to our world,
that all nations may see and hear.[8]

In obedience to the truth may our lives be pure,
growing in genuine, mutual love.[9]

≈

May your word be at work in all believers,
enabling acceptance in depth.
For the word we accepted is no human word.
It is God's word at work in us.[10]

References

(1)   Rom 10:16, 17   (2)   Mt 13:14, 15
(3)   Mt 11:4   (4)   Heb 3:8-10
(5)   Heb 4:1, 2   (6)   Mk 9:7
(7)   Rom 1:3-5   (8)   Acts 2:17-21
(9)   1 Pet 1:22   (10) 1 Thess 2:13

*L*oving God

The new commandment invites us to love God in and through loving others.

God, you have given us, through Jesus, a new
    commandment.
Help us to love one another as Jesus has loved us.[1]

By the love I have for others
let me be recognized as a disciple of Jesus.[2]

Grace me to rejoice when others rejoice
and to be sad with those in sorrow.[3]

Make our Church one group of believers,
united, like the early Christians, in heart and soul,[4]
knowing we can have no greater love
than to lay down our lives for our friends.[5]

According to the grace that was given to each,
let me use my gifts in service,
aiming to be rich in all those gifts
that go to build up the community.[6]

Love is the greatest of all the gifts –
patient, kind, rejoicing in the truth,
ready to make allowances,
to endure whatever comes.
Love never comes to an end.[7]

Spirit of God, make firm my inner self.
May Christ live in my heart through faith,
that I may be planted in and built on love.[8]

≈

What I do to the least of your people,
to you, God, it is also done.[9]

≈

For the sake of your glory,
let me accept all others
as Christ has accepted me.[10]

References

(1) Jn 13:34   (2) Jn 13:35
(3) Rom 12:15   (4) Acts 4:32
(5) Jn 15:13   (6) 1 Cor 12:4-11 & 13:4-8
(7) 1 Cor 13:13 & 13:4-8 (8) Eph 3:16-19
(9) Mt 25:33-40   (10) Rom 15:7

*M*agdalene

Magdalene is a model of mercy received and of love returned. She was the first person chosen by Christ to proclaim his resurrection.

 I thank you, God, for your grace in Magdalene,
cleansing her to love you as she did.[1]

May I follow you to Calvary in love,
as Magdalene and the other women did.[2]

Gift me with her repentant love,
she who came to the tomb with sadness and hope.[3]

As she wept, seeing the emptiness there,
may I also weep when Jesus seems absent.[4]

Jesus, I know you call me by name.
May I find you in every person.[5]

Make strong my hope in my own resurrection
so that I too will one day say 'I have seen the
Lord.'[6]

When disbelief is the response to my words,
keep me firm and steeped in faith.[7]

With courage, I can overcome all human respect
and make concrete my good intentions.[8]

Through the loyalty of Magdalene who stood by
　　the cross,
may my faith and trust endure to the end.[9]

～

And when asked at death 'Who do you seek?'
I will answer 'The risen Christ,'
making my joy complete.[10]

References

(1)	Lk 8:1, 2	(2)	Mt 27:56
(3)	Jn 20:1	(4)	Lk 24:3
(5)	Jn 20:16	(6)	Jn 20:18
(7)	Lk 24:11	(8)	Jn 11:3
(9)	Jn 19:25	(10)	Jn 20:15

M*arriage*

Marriage is ideally a covenant relationship of total fidelity between man and woman.

 God, lead us to hold your gift of marriage in high
      honor
  – a covenant undefiled and faithful.[1]

For you created male and female,
husband and wife living together as one.
A union so sacred, inseparable.[2]

Just as woman came from man
so man came through woman
– each dependent on the other,
but all things come from you.[3]

Enable husbands to love their wives
and to treat them with gentleness,[4]
loving them as Christ loved the Church
when he gave himself up for her.[5]

Enable wives to respect their husbands,[6]
and deepen the awareness of each
to the other's needs and limitations,
remembering that both are heirs
to the gracious gift of life.[7]

Make their homes, God, places of welcome
with the warm hospitality of Martha.[8]

And may their children increase in wisdom and
      years,
in divine and human favor.[9]

≈

Marriage, a profound mystery
– two becoming one,
imaging Christ and his Church.[10]

References

(1)	Heb 13:4	(2)	Mt 19:4-6
(3)	1 Cor 11:12	(4)	Col 3:19
(5)	Eph 5:25	(6)	Eph 5:33
(7)	1 Pet 3:7	(8)	Lk 10:38
(9)	Lk 2:52	(10)	Eph 5:32

M*ary*

Mary is a model of faith in her openness to God's invitation and in her fidelity to the end.

 'Greetings, favoured one! The Lord is with you.'
'The power of the Most High will overshadow you.'[1]

God, give me the faith of Mary who believed.
Renew me, like Elizabeth, with the fullness of your
    Spirit.[2]

The word became flesh and lived among us.
May my heart be open to receive him anew.[3]

Like Mary's child, Jesus, may all children grow
    strong,
filled with wisdom and enjoying your favor.[4]

In times of anxiety and failure to understand,
let me treasure, like Mary, your word in my heart.[5]

Mary, you have been given to me.
May I, like John, take you into my home.[6]

I remember your words spoken at Cana:
'Do whatever he tells you.'[7]

When trial and suffering are part of my life,
help me to bear the sword that pierces.[8]

≈

As Mary tended your needs with love,
help me, Jesus, in my caring.[9]

≈

She prayed with the united early Church.
Let unity and prayer mark your Church today.[10]

References

(1)	Lk 1:26-35	(2)	Lk 1:39-45
(3)	Jn 1:14	(4)	Lk 2:40
(5)	Lk 2:42-52	(6)	Jn 19:26, 27
(7)	Jn 2:1-11	(8)	Lk 2:34, 35
(9)	Jn 19:23, 24	(10)	Acts 1:14

M*eals*

In scripture, meals were symbols of fellowship. They were celebrations of mutual acceptance and friendship.

 Jesus, you gave the first of your signs
at the wedding feast of Cana.[1]

You joined in the banquet given by Levi,
accepting all who were present.[2]

In compassion, you shared the loaves and the fish.
The people all ate and were filled.[3]

Forgiveness was given and a woman loved
in the Pharisee's house at table.[4]

You asked for a drink at Jacob's well
and spoke of the water of life.[5]

You joined in the dinner served by Martha
at the home of your Bethany friends.[6]

Taking the bread, you broke it.
Taking the cup, you gave thanks.[7]

Your disciples, disbelieving and wondering still,
saw you eat in their presence.[8]

And you opened the eyes of the travellers to
    Emmaus,
at table breaking bread.[9]

꧅

The breakfast you served from the charcoal fire
was enjoyed by your weary disciples.
Let me cherish our times of leisure and quiet,
our times for eating and resting together.[10]

꧅

And blessed will I be when I hear the words:
'Blessed are those who are invited to the marriage
    feast of the Lamb.'[11]

References

(1) Jn 2:1-11   (2) Lk 5:29
(3) Lk 9:12-17   (4) Lk 7:36-50
(5) Jn 4:7-14   (6) Jn 12:1, 2
(7) Lk 22:14-20   (8) Lk 24:41-43
(9) Lk 24:30, 31   (10) Jn 21:3-11 & Mk 6:31, 32
(11) Rev 19:9

M*ercy*

Mercy is the permanent expression of God's love and tenderness for us when we sin. We pass on the same mercy to one another, as Jesus reminds us to do in the words of the 'Our Father.'

 God, I know that our hearts must always forgive,
not seven times only but again and again.[1]

A repentant heart must always be forgiven.
Give me grace to respond to the asking.[2]

Your mercy is from generation to generation
for those who revere you.
May I always know that your mercy is mine.[3]

Help me to bear with others in their weakness
and to forgive them just as you forgive me.[4]

I thank you, God, for rescuing me from the power
of darkness
and transferring me into the kingdom of your Son.
In him I have redemption – my sins forgiven.[5]

By your tender mercy, God,
the dawn from on high has visited me.[6]

Make me perfect in merciful loving
as you, God of heaven, are perfect.[7]

May I, like the Baptist, prepare the way
so that all can know your salvation
and experience your forgiveness.[8]

≈

I know that I am among the blessed
– that because I show mercy
I will receive it.[9]

References

(1) Mt 18:21, 22   (2) Lk 17:4
(3) Lk 1:50   (4) Col 3:13
(5) Col 1:13, 14   (6) Lk 1:76-78
(7) Mt 5:48   (8) Lk 1:76-78
(9) Mt 5:7

M iracle

There are everyday miracles worked by love, and special ones, which are rare.
For people of faith, miracles great and small are signs of God's presence.

 God, give me the faith that enables miracles.
You healed the paralytic through the faith of his
friends.[1]

Help me in accepting whatever you plan.
The leper was cured; he left all in your hands.[2]

Let me step out in faith, with absolute trust,
walking like Jesus the waters of life.[3]

Never allow others to struggle in pain
because of my absence or weakness of faith.[4]

May I know, God, your presence amidst the noise
of our world.
Like the blind man of Jericho, you will hear and
have pity.[5]

Make radical my faith, Jesus.
Give me the courage of the woman
who touched the fringe of your cloak.[6]

The five thousand were fed with love and
compassion.
May I always be ready to share what I have.[7]

In total humility, like the Canaanite woman
let me own my sinfulness and accept all as gift.[8]

≈

Deepen in me, God, the freedom of Jesus,
that when faced with others' needs
I will not be enslaved by the letter of the law.[9]

≈

Like the centurion who loved his servant,
make me deeply aware that all life is sacred.[10]

References

(1)	Mt 9:1-8	(2)	Mt 8:1-4
(3)	Mt 14:22-33	(4)	Mt 17:14-20
(5)	Mt 20:29-34	(6)	Mt 9:18-26
(7)	Mt 14:13-21	(8)	Mt 15:22-28
(9)	Mt 12:9-14	(10)	Mt 8:5-13

M ission

Each one of us has unique gifts and we are asked to use them in building up the reign of God.

 God, give me grace to accept your plan,
courage to carry out my mission to the end.[1]

John, you were on mission in the wilderness,
helping people to see God's salvation.[2]

Mary, you conceived and bore a son
'Let it be with me according to your word.'[3]

Joseph, you took Mary as your wife
and fostered her son Jesus.[4]

Jesus, you brought the good news to the poor,
release to the captives and sight to the blind.[5]

Jesus, let me hear once again, your words: 'Follow me.'
Deepen my commitment to mission,
leaving anew all that I have
– ready for total giving.[6]

Call me each moment to be your disciple,
sending me out to proclaim the message.[7]

With Peter, let me say: 'To whom can we go?
You have the words of eternal life.'[8]

You have shone in my heart, God,
and given me the knowledge of your own glory,
the glory on the face of Christ.[9]

References

(1)	2 Tim 4:6-8	(2)	Jn 1:19-23
(3)	Lk 1:38	(4)	Mt 1:18-25
(5)	Lk 4:17, 18	(6)	Mt 4:18-22
(7)	Mk 16:14, 15	(8)	Jn 6:67-69
(9)	2 Cor 4:6		

M otherhood

God loves us as a mother loves the child in her womb. Reflecting God's
motherly love, all motherhood is the privilege to freely give and nurture life.

 God, in motherliness you gather your children
as a hen gathers her brood beneath her wings.[1]

Send your Holy Spirit upon all mothers.
Overshadow them with your power.[2]

Deepen their faith and make it sincere,
like the faith of their mothers before them.[3]

Give them fidelity in their suffering
when pierced with the sword of pain.[4]

And hear their pleas for your healing touch
for children sick and ailing.[5]

Walk with mothers in times of loss
gently easing their grieving.[6]

Temper their ambition and keep them from evil.
Draw them to deeper conversion.[7]

Help mothers cherish their childen as gifts.
Ready are they for the kingdom.[8]

And deepen my reverence for the sacredness of life,
knowing you are the God of all.[9]

References

(1) Lk 13:34   (2) Lk 1:35
(3) 2 Tim 1:5   (4) Lk 2:33-35 & Jn 19:25
(5) Mk 7:24-30   (6) Lk 7:11-15
(7) Mt 20:20-22 & 27:56
(8) Lk 18:15, 16   (9) Lk 1:25

*O*bedience

Biblical obedience is an adult willingness to receive God's liberating word and to live it.

 God, your Son Jesus came into this world to carry
out your will.
And so, through the offering of his body for all,
we have now been sanctified.[1]

❧

Jesus, you spoke of God's will as food.
Sustain me as I work.
Nourish my resolve to do God's will,
God's teaching, not my own.[2]

❧

I will never be lost or forgotten
for to Jesus I have been given.
Let me see your Son, God, in whom I believe.
Raise me to life eternal.[3]

❧

I know that Jesus' obedience to you
was the source of his power to act.
Empower me, God, with your own Spirit.
Draw me to oneness of will with you.[4]

❧

Let my mind be the same as the mind of Christ
Jesus
– a total emptying of self,
obedient to death, death on a cross.
May his dying be my strength.[5]

❧

I do nothing on my own, said Jesus,
only as the Father has told me.
God, bring my will into harmony with yours
even on my way to Gethsemane.[6]

❧

Through my pain may I learn obedience,
submitting in reverence and in trust.[7]
'Not my will but yours be done'
– two wills merging as one.[8]

❧

Like Jesus, you never leave me alone.
May I do what is pleasing to you,[9]
glorifying you by completing my mission,
the work you give me to do.[10]

References

(1)	Heb 10:5-10	(2)	Jn 4:34 &. 7:17
(3)	Jn 6.38-40	(4)	Mt 8:9
(5)	Phil 2:5-8	(6)	Jn 5:30 & 14:31
(7)	Heb 5:7, 8	(8)	Lk 22:42
(9)	Jn 8:28, 29	(10)	Jn 17:4

*P*atience

God's patience with us is the inspiration for our acceptance of ourselves and of others. It is the fruit of the Holy Spirit.

 Spirit of God, nurture within me your fruits
– love, peace, patience.[1]

❧

As your holy ones, beloved and chosen,
clothe me with patience in bearing with others.[2]

❧

I want to live a life worthy of my calling,
with humility, gentleness and patience.[3]

❧

As the farmer waits for the crop to grow
and patiently hopes for early and late rains,
give me the grace to wait in patience
for the day of your own coming.[4]

❧

With you, God, a thousand years are like a single day.
Be patient with me and with our world,
enabling salvation for everyone.[5]

❧

Make me strong with the strength of your power,
that I may endure everything with patience,[6]
imitating those who through faith and patience
are able to inherit the promises.[7]

❧

Let me never disregard the riches of God's kindness
– goodness, forbearance and patience.[8]

In admonishing, encouraging and helping others,
gift me with patience for all.[9]

Steep me in Jesus' own patience towards me,
on my journey to life eternal.[10]

References

(1)	1 Cor 13:4	(2)	Col 3:12, 13
(3)	Eph 4:1-3	(4)	Jas 5:7-11
(5)	2 Pet 3:8, 9	(6)	Col 1:11, 12
(7)	Heb 6:11, 12	(8)	Rom 2:1-7
(9)	1 Thess 5:14	(10)	1 Tim 1:16

Paul

After his conversion, Paul described his life in these words: 'I live, no longer I, but Christ lives in me.'

 'Who are you, Lord?' asked the shattered Saul.
'I am Jesus, whom you are persecuting.'[1]

Paul, servant of God and apostle of Christ,
shares with me the grace and peace he has received.[2]

With Paul, I remember and pray for others,
giving thanks to God for the joy we share.[3]

Help me, God, to become all things to all people,
that all may partake of the blessings of the Gospel.[4]

May we strengthen one another with some spiritual
    gift,
and yearn like Paul for the sharing of our faith.[5]

I know that Christ Jesus has made me his own,
and I strain towards the goal to which I am called.[5]

I carry in my body the death of Jesus
so that his life too may be visible in me.[6]

The tent I now live in will be destroyed.
I long to be clothed with my heavenly dwelling.[8]

≫

May I come to regard all things as loss
because of the value of knowing Christ Jesus.[9]

≫

When the time draws near for me to be gone,
may I also, with Paul, have kept the faith.[10]

References

(1) Acts 9:5
(2) Titus 1:1-4
(3) Phil 1:3
(4) 1 Cor 9:19-23
(5) Rom 1:11, 12
(6) Phil 3:12-16
(7) 2 Cor 4:10
(8) 2 Cor 5:1-3
(9) Phil 3:8
(10) 2 Tim 4:6-8

Peace

The Spirit's gift of peace grows from our reconciliation with God, with ourselves, with others and with respect for our environment.

 God, you have called us to peace
– peace with one another.[1]

May Christ's peace reign in our hearts;
to this we are called in one body.[2]

Let me then seek peace and pursue it ever,
for my God is a God of peace.[3]

It is through Jesus that I have peace with you,
for he, the Christ, is my peace.[4]

May we be entirely one new humanity
– sanctified, reconciled, at peace.[5]

For your kingdom, God, is not food and drink
but righteousness, peace and joy in the Spirit.[6]

Let me be a peacemaker, a child of God,
pursuing what makes for mutual up-building.[7]

Abounding in hope by the power of your spirit,
may I know joy and peace in believing.[8]

Give to our world peace in abundance.
I long to be in Christ Jesus.[9]

≈

Jesus, you have given your peace to me.
May I never be troubled or afraid.[10]

References

(1) 1 Cor 7:15 & Mk 9:50   (2) Col 3:15
(3) 1 Pet 3:11 & 1 Cor 14:33 (4) Rom 5:1, 2 & Eph 2:14
(5) Eph 2:15-18 & 1 Thess 5:23
(6) Rom 14:17   (7) Mt 5:9 & Rom 14:19
(8) Rom 15:13   (9) Jude v. 2 & 1 Pet 5:14
(10) Jn 14:27

*P*erseverance

Fidelity to our goals demands commitment and perseverance in the everyday struggles of life.

 Merciful God, you know our weakness,
and the test will never be beyond our strength.[1]

As Jesus suffered and left an example,
give me strength to follow his steps.[2]

Support me in every hardship, God,
that I in turn may support others.[3]

May I proclaim Jesus – a crucified Christ,
but also the power and the wisdom of God.[4]

Give me perseverance; deepen my faith,
that I may be worthy of your kingdom.[5]

If I have died with Jesus,
I shall live with him,
and if I have endured with Jesus,
I shall also reign with him.[6]

For Christ suffered once for the sin of the world,
that he might lead all people to you.[7]

As Jesus, the innocent, died for all,
may my life be upright: may I die to my sins.[8]

Increase my trust as you allow me to suffer,
witnessing always to the suffering of Christ.[9]

≫

With the sufferings I bear, the encouragement I
    share,
in this knowledge, God, may my hope be secure.[10]

References

(1)	1 Cor 10:13	(2)	1 Pet 2:21
(3)	2 Cor 1:4	(4)	1 Cor 1:22-24
(5)	2 Thess 1:4, 5	(6)	2 Tim 2:11, 12
(7)	1 Pet 3:18	(8)	1 Pet 2:20-25
(9)	1 Pet 4:12-19	(10)	2 Cor 1:7

P*eter*

*Peter was chosen by Jesus. In moments of trial he failed, but in his sorrow
Jesus forgave him. He died a martyr.*

 God, after the example of Peter and the apostles,
let me also leave what I have and follow Jesus.[1]

Set my mind on the things that are divine
– not on human things.[2]

Deepen the little faith that I have.
I know Jesus is truly your Son.[3]

Strengthen my weakness, make willing my spirit
to watch and pray in times of distress.[4]

Bring me, like Peter, to own my sinfulness
as I stand in awe at your wonders.[5]

With him I make my profession of faith:
Jesus has the words of eternal life.
He is the holy one in whom I believe.
God, to whom else can I go?[6]

Jesus, take me to the mountain top;
give me a glimpse of your glory.
It is good for me to be here with you.
I long to remain in your presence.[7]

Gift me with total conversion of heart
as I weep for myself and our world.[8]

&

Confident in the healing power of your spirit,
may I reach out to those in affliction.[9]

&

Like Peter, unbind the chains that enslave me.
Open the gates to my freedom.[10]

References

(1)	Mt 4:18-20	(2)	Mt 16:21-23
(3)	Mt 14:28-33	(4)	Mt 26:40, 41
(5)	Lk 5:4-8	(6)	Jn 6:66-69
(7)	Mt 17:1-4	(8)	Mt 26:69-75
(9)	Acts 3:6, 7	(10)	Acts 12:6-11

*P*ossessions

All things are good and God made them for our shared happiness. However, there is always the risk that these gifts might possess or enslave us.

 'She out of her poverty has put in everything
she had, all she had to live on.'[1]

Bring me, God, to cheerfulness in giving,
sharing abundantly in every good work.[2]

You have given me your spirit and anointed me
to bring good news to the poor.[3]

For the poor we will always have with us.
They are blessed, for the kingdom is theirs.[4]

You look on me, Jesus, with deep love.
Make total my following of you.[5]

Ready me, God, to share my resources
– spiritual blessings and material things.[6]

Let me not worry about my life and its needs
but rather strive first for the kingdom.[7]

Put me on guard against all kinds of greed;
from abundance of possessions unclutter me.[8]

You have chosen me, God, as an heir to the
     kingdom.
Bring me to Gospel poverty and to richness in
     faith.[9]

≈

May your love abide in my heart, I pray,
as I love in truth and action.[10]

References

(1) Mk 12:43, 44   (2) 2 Cor 9:7-9
(3) Lk 4:18   (4) Mk 14:7 & Lk 6:20
(5) Mk 10:21, 22   (6) Rom 15:25-27
(7) Mt 6:25-33   (8) Lk 12:15
(9) Jas 2:5   (10) 1 Jn 3:17-18

*P*rayer

Prayer is the great religious act. It is a willingness to be still and know that God is 'Abba.'

 Holy Spirit, help me in my weakness.
You pray for me in accordance with the mind of
   God.[1]

Ꙅ

While rejoicing in hope and patient in suffering,
grace me, God, to persevere in prayer.[2]

Ꙅ

Help me to pray as your Son prayed,
that your name be held holy.[3]

Ꙅ

At all times I pray in your Holy Spirit,
making supplication for all.[4]

Ꙅ

In cheerfulness, I sing songs of praise,
in sickness, I pray the prayer of anointing,
praying with faith and for one another.
The prayer of the righteous is powerful.[5]

Ꙅ

All your creation, God, is good.
Let me receive with thanksgiving,
for all is sanctified by your word.
Be with me in my prayer.[6]

Ꙅ

Devoting myself to the word and to fellowship,
to the breaking of bread and the prayers.[7]

Ꙅ

If we ask, it will be given to us.
In searching we will find.
Knocking will open the door for us
– all in Jesus' name.[8]

I pray, God, that your word may spread,
that everywhere you may be glorified.[9]

May my prayer and alms ascend before you
and may the prayers of many bring blessings.[10]

References

(1) Rom 8:26, 27

(2) Rom 12:13

(3) Lk 11:1-4

(4) Eph 6:18 & 1 Tim 2:1, 2

(5) Jas 5:13-16

(6) 1 Tim 4:4, 5

(7) Acts 2:42

(8) Mt 7:7-11 & Jn 14:13

(9) 2 Thess 3:1, 2

(10) 2 Cor 1:11 & Acts 10:31

*P*urity of Heart

Biblical purity is singlemindedness in the search for God.

 Let me walk in the light together with others
and the blood of Jesus will cleanse me from all sin.[1]

Draw near to me, God, as I draw near to you.
Cleanse my hands and purify my heart.[2]

You call me, not to impurity but to holiness.
May I never reject your authority
or the gift of your Holy Spirit.[3]

By obedience to the truth, may my soul be purified,
so that genuine mutual love may be mine.[4]

Purify my conscience from the dead works of sin.
Through the blood of Christ and the eternal Spirit,
may I offer my worship to you.[5]

I want to be like you, my God,
when I see you as you are.
Purify me then just as you are pure.[6]

I must remember that I am a child of light, of the
    day;
I am not of the night or of darkness.[7]

As though reflected in a mirror, I see your glory,
   God.
Gently transform me into this same glory
through the power of your Holy Spirit.[8]

～

May the cunning of evil never lead me astray.
Gift me with sincere and pure devotion to Christ.[9]

～

You have called me with a holy calling
according to your own purpose and grace revealed
   in Jesus
– Jesus, who abolished death and brought life
and immortality through the Gospel.[10]

References

(1)	1 Jn 1:7	(2)	Jas 4:8
(3)	1 Thess 4:7, 8	(4)	1 Pet 1:22
(5)	Heb 9:13, 14	(6)	1 Jn 3:2, 3
(7)	1 Thess 5:4-8	(8)	2 Cor 3:18
(9)	2 Cor 11:3	(10)	2 Tim 1:8-10

*R*econciliation

Reconciliation is the healing of a broken friendship. God always offers us this gift and we share it with others.

 Even while we were enemies,
we were reconciled to you, God,
through the death of your Son.[1]

I thank you for reconciling all things to yourself,
things on earth and things in heaven,
making peace through the blood of Christ.[2]

Yes, truly I have known salvation
by the forgiveness of my sins,
and by your tender mercy, God,
the dawn from on high has broken upon me.[3]

Make me perfect in merciful loving,
just as you are merciful.[4]

You have rescued me from the power of darkness
and transferred me into the kingdom of your Son.[5]

I, who was once estranged and hostile, am now
reconciled.
Make steadfast my faith.[6]

Strengthen me, God, in my ministry of
    reconciliation,
that I do not accept your grace in vain.[7]

≈≈≈

Like Jesus, let me sympathize with human
    weakness,
Jesus who was tested in all ways, like me.[8]

≈≈≈

I rejoice in celebration when forgiveness is given,
when the lost are found and death becomes life.[9]

≈≈≈

I know always that, where sin increased,
grace abounded all the more.[10]

References

(1)	Rom 5:10	(2)	Col 1:19, 20
(3)	Lk 1:76-78	(4)	Lk 6:36
(5)	Col 1:13, 14	(6)	Col 1:21-23
(7)	2 Cor 5:17-6:1	(8)	Heb 4:15, 16
(9)	Lk 15:11-32	(10)	Rom 5:20

Redemption

Through Jesus, God has redeemed us. In Jesus, the sinless one, we become the very holiness of God.

 I bless you, God.
You looked on us with favor
and redeemed us through Jesus, a mighty savior.[1]

The blessing of Abraham has come to us
and we have received the promise of the Spirit
    through you.[2]

Disregarding the shame, you endured the cross.
Help me, your disciple, to take up my cross,
to deny myself and to follow you.[3]

Bring me, God, to pray in truth
– with Christ I have been crucified,
and now no longer do I live,
but Christ lives in me.[4]

I have shared in your Holy Spirit
and tasted the goodness of the word.
Let me never fall away
and crucify again your Son Jesus, the Christ.[5]

Having made peace through the blood of his cross,
all things are now reconciled,
for the fullness of your Godhead dwelt in Jesus.
May I too dwell in him.[6]

My ransom not with things that perish,
not with gold and silver,
but the precious blood of Jesus Christ,
the lamb without spot or blemish.[7]

≈

You have rescued me, God, from the power of
    darkness,
and transferred me to the kingdom of your Son,
your Son the beloved, in whom I am redeemed,
in whom I am forgiven.[8]

References

(1) Lk 1:68, 69   (2) Gal 3:13, 14
(3) Heb 12:2 & Mt 16:24, 25
(4) Gal 2:20   (5) Heb 6:5, 6
(6) Col 1:19, 20   (7) 1 Pet 1:18, 19
(8) Col 1:13-14

Repentance

We repent when we recognize our sinfulness and allow God to immerse us in his merciful love.

 The time is fulfilled and the kingdom of God has
   come near.
Repent and believe the Good News.[1]

❧

Grace me God; I need to change.
Gift me with childlike trust and surrender.[2]

❧

Make generous my turning to you in love,
remembering you first turned to me.[3]

❧

Let me proclaim in your name to all the nations
the message of repentance – the forgiveness of sins.[4]

❧

You exalted Jesus as Leader and Savior,
that I might be gifted with repentance and
   forgiveness.[5]

❧

Open my being to the Spirit of Jesus,
that all I meet may become a converted people.[6]

❧

May all people turn from darkness to light,
from the power of Satan to the holiness of God,
and be placed among those who are sanctified by
   faith.[7]

❧

That times of refreshment may come to me
from the presence of Jesus among us,
deepen my turning to you each day
as I move towards total sinlessness.[8]

❧

Soften my disregard of your abundant goodness.
May I realize that your kindness leads to
    repentance.[9]

❧

Fill the void of human ignorance, God,
enabling repentance for all.[10]

References

(1)	Mk 1:14, 15	(2)	Mt 18:3, 4
(3)	1 Jn 4:19	(4)	Lk 24:47
(5)	Acts 5:31	(6)	Lk 4:18
(7)	Acts 26:18	(8)	Acts 3:19, 20
(9)	Rom 2:4, 5	(10)	Acts 17:30

Resurrection

Our faith rests on God's promise that, in the resurrection of Jesus, we too will rise again.

 God, your Son Jesus, in accordance with your will,
laid down his life to take it up again.[1]

I am a witness to his resurrection as the first
    apostles were.
Grace me to proclaim Jesus, the risen Lord.[2]

You raised Jesus from death.
To be held in its power was impossible for him.[3]

Christ then is the first fruit of my redemption.[4]

He is the head of the body, the Church,
the beginning, the first born from the dead.
First place is his – in everything.[5]

May I hand on to all what I have received:
Christ's death for our sins;
his rising the third day;
his appearance to the twelve;
the scriptures fulfilled.[6]

In Baptism I was buried with Jesus
and, through faith in God's power,
I was also raised with him.[7]

PRAYING THE NEW TESTAMENT AS PSALMS

As Christ was raised by the glory of the Father,
so I too might walk in newness of life.[8]

⁂

All I want is to know Christ and the power of his
    rising,
to share his sufferings,
to become like him in his death,
that somehow I may attain resurrection.[9]

⁂

Hearing the word through Jesus
and believing that God sent him
is my passage from death to life.[10]

References

(1)	Jn 10:17, 18	(2)	Acts 1:22
(3)	Acts 2:23, 24	(4)	1 Cor 15:20
(5)	Col 1:18	(6)	1 Cor 15:3-5
(7)	Col 2:12	(8)	Rom 6:3-6
(9)	Phil 3:10, 11	(10)	Jn 5:24

Sacrifice

In the New Testament, sacrifice is the willingness to give our lives to God, as Jesus did. It is an act of trust and self-surrender based on faith.

 Our paschal Lamb, Christ, has been sacrificed.
Let me celebrate the festival
with the unleavened bread of sincerity and truth.[1]

As a beloved child, may I be an imitator of God
and live in love as Christ loved me.
He gave himself up – a fragrant offering,
a sacrifice to you, God, for me.[2]

Let me offer my body as a living sacrifice,
holy, acceptable – my spiritual worship.[3]

Build us, God, into a spiritual house, a holy
        priesthood,
offering spiritual sacrifices acceptable to you
        through Christ.[4]

I know that you have removed all sin
by the sacrifice of Jesus, your Son.[5]

Grace me to do good and to share what I have.
Such sacrifices are pleasing to you.[6]

Through Jesus I continually offer a sacrifice of praise,
the fruit of lips that confess his name.[7]

≋

May the gifts we send be a fragrant offering,
a sacrifice acceptable and pleasing.[8]

≋

For you, God, will satisfy my every need
according to your riches glorious in Christ.[9]

References

(1)	1 Cor 5:7, 8	(2)	Eph 5:1, 2
(3)	Rom 12:1	(4)	1 Pet 2:4, 5
(5)	Heb 9:26	(6)	Heb 13:16
(7)	Heb 13:15	(8)	Eph 5:2
(9)	Phil 4:19		

S *alvation*

Salvation is freedom from everything that oppresses the human person and especially freedom from sin.

 Salvation belongs to our God, who is seated on the
    throne,
and to the lamb.[1]

❧

God, you have looked favorably on your people
and redeemed them.[2]

❧

You send me to give knowledge of salvation to all
by the forgiveness of their sins.[3]

❧

For I know that if I lose my life for your sake and
    the Gospel,
I will save it.[4]

❧

I have been justified by the blood of Jesus
and in hope I am saved.[5]

❧

He will transform my humble body
and conform it to the body of his glory.
My citizenship is in heaven.[6]

❧

I have heard the word of truth, the Gospel of my
    salvation,
and been marked with the seal of the Holy Spirit,
the pledge of my inheritance.[7]

❧

Acknowledging all as your gift to me,
by grace I have been saved.[8]

≈

I rejoice with a joy indescribable and glorious
at the outcome of my faith
– the salvation of my soul.[9]

≈

As I wait for the promised new heaven and new
    earth,
let me be found at peace without spot or blemish,
regarding the patience of my God as salvation.[10]

References

(1) Rev 7:9, 10   (2) Lk 1:68, 69
(3) Lk 1:77   (4) Mk 8:35
(5) Rom 5:9 & 8:24   (6) Phil 3:20, 21
(7) Eph 1:13, 14   (8) Eph 2:5-9
(9) 1 Pet 1:8, 9   (10) 2 Pet 3:13-15

*S*elf-Transcendence

Human growth and Christian fulfillment involve rising above and becoming liberated from anything that might limit our inner freedom.

 God, in your love,
free me from over-attachment to life.[1]

❦

As you gently invite me to restful quiet,
from the lure of activity free me.[2]

❦

In moments of suffering, doubt and pain,
merge my self-concern into grief for others.[3]

❦

Unclutter my life of material things,
enabling greater likeness to Jesus.[4]

❦

From resentment and unforgiveness,
heal me, God, that I may call the other 'friend.'[5]

❦

All people are equal in your sight.
Cleanse my heart of racist tendencies.[6]

❦

Power for Christ meant enablement.
Let me never see power as dominance.[7]

❦

In the courage of your Spirit, may I live out my
    mission
in spite of all threats and intimidation.[8]

❦

That I may grow into the sinless Christ,
touch me in my sinfulness.[9]

References

(1) Jn 10:17, 18
(2) Mk 6:30, 31
(3) Jn 19:26, 27
(4) Lk 9:58
(5) Mt 26:49, 50
(6) Jn 4:9
(7) Jn 6:15
(8) Lk 13:31, 32
(9) Jn 8:46

S*haring*

Authentic love implies sharing our material and spiritual gifts with those who are in need, just as God shares endlessly with us.

 God, in sharing with us your glory through Jesus,
may we be one as you and he are one.[1]

Deepen in me the grace of Jesus,
your own love and the communion of your Spirit.[2]

Keep me from the corruption that is in the world,
as I become a participant in your divine nature.[3]

Make me eager to share what I have.
Such sacrifices are pleasing to you.[4]

Let me see my sharing as truly a privilege,
grateful for everything as gift.[5]

I want to become all things to all people,
for the sake of the Gospel
and to share in its blessings.[6]

In the blood of Jesus we share.
We share in the body of Christ.
One bread, one body, in Eucharist we partake.[7]

If I have died with Jesus, I shall also live with him,
and if I endure I will reign to share in his
resurrection.[8]

≈

Bring me to know Christ and the power of his rising,
to share in his sufferings, to become like him in his
death.[9]

≈

I pray that the sharing of my faith be effective,
knowing all the good I may do for Christ.[10]

References

(1)	Jn 17:21, 22	(2)	2 Cor 13:13
(3)	2 Pet 1:4	(4)	2 Cor 8:3, 4
(5)	Heb 13:16	(6)	1 Cor 9:22
(7)	1 Cor 10:16-17	(8)	2 Tim 2:11-13
(9)	Phil 3:10	(10)	Philem v. 6

S*in*

Sin is a turning away from God when we fail to accept God's unconditional love and when we refuse to love ourselves or others with that love. In this way, we lessen or destroy our relationship with God, thus harming ourselves.

 Let me never say, God, that I have not sinned,
or I make you a liar and your word is not in me.[1]

≫

Rather I present myself as a slave of obedience,
which leads me to righteousness,
not a slave of sin, which leads to death.[2]

≫

I am set free from sin and am bound to your service.
Deepen this freedom within me
and strengthen my commitment.[3]

≫

I have met Jesus – encountered the Christ;
may I never refuse to believe in him.[4]

≫

My former self was crucified with Christ
and through this dying I am freed from sin.[5]

≫

Help me to believe the message of Jesus,
that I may have eternal life.[6]

≫

May I not let sin reign over my body
making it an instrument of evil.[7]

≫

I have already died to sin,
so how could I go on living in it?[8]

⁓

Rescue me, God, from the body of this death.
as I give thanks to you through Jesus.[9]

⁓

Make me free with the freedom of your Son.
Then I will be free indeed.[10]

References

(1)   1 Jn 1:10   (2)   Rom 6:16
(3)   Rom 6:22   (4)   Jn 16:8,9
(5)   Rom 6:6, 7   (6)   Jn 3:36
(7)   Rom 6:12, 13   (8)   Rom 6:1, 2
(9)   Rom 7:22-25   (10) Jn 8:34-36

S*incerity*

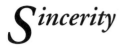

To be sincere is to be open, honest, straightforward and without guile – like God.

 God, we are like sheep in the midst of wolves.
Make me wise as a serpent and simple as a dove.[1]

Keep me chaste with the spiritual virginity of
    single-mindedness,
with a sincere and pure devotion to Christ.[2]

Change me, God, to become like a child.
Make me humble, that I may enter the kingdom.[3]

In welcoming those who are least among all
– they are the greatest – I welcome you, God.[4]

I do not celebrate with the yeast of malice
but with the unleavened bread of sincerity and
    truth.[5]

Sent by you, God, I stand in your presence,[6]
speaking as a person of sincerity in Christ.

Let me behave with frankness and godly sincerity,
not by earthly wisdom but by your grace.[7]

Rid me, God, of all malice and guile,
all envy, insincerity and anger,
longing for the pure, spiritual milk
that nourishes growth into salvation.[8]

≈

Indeed, my heart is in the testimony of my
    conscience.
May I never become false, deceitful, disguised.[9]

≈

Open my heart to embrace everyone.
May their hearts be open to receive my affection.[10]

References

(1)	Mt 10:16	(2)	2 Cor 11:2, 3
(3)	Mt 18:1-4	(4)	Lk 9:46-48
(5)	1 Cor 5:6-8	(6)	2 Cor 2:17
(7)	2 Cor 1:12	(8)	1 Pet 2:1-3
(9)	2 Cor 1:12 & 11:13, 14	(10)	2 Cor 6:11-13

*S*ocial Justice

Social justice exists when all people and groups of people have their God-given human rights respected.

 'Blessed are those who hunger and thirst for
    righteousness,
for they will be filled.'¹

I remember that you, God, have chosen the poor to
    be rich in faith.
May I never dishonor them.²

Deepen in me my love for my neighbor
as I carry out the works that accompany faith.³

As a believer in Jesus, let me never make
    distinctions
nor with evil thoughts become a judge over others.⁴

Give me wisdom, pure, from above,
without trace of partiality,
make me peaceable, gentle.⁵

Help me to bring forth a harvest of righteousness,
sown in peace by those who make peace.⁶

Let me not set my heart on silver and gold,
living in luxury and pleasure,
but aim at justice in my dealings with others,
not greed at their expense.[7]

❧

Call me anew, God, to the making of peace.
Blessed are the peacemakers, your children.[8]

❧

Show me your strength and scatter my pride.
Convert my power into lowliness.[9]

❧

Let me see the injustice of our world
and join you in raising up the lowly.[10]

❧

Let me boast, in my lowliness, of being raised up.
Make generous all of my giving.[11]

References

(1)   Mt 5:6
(2)   Jas 2:5, 6
(3)   Jas 2:15-17
(4)   Jas 2:1-4
(5)   Jas 3:17
(6)   Jas 3:18
(7)   Jas 5:1-6
(8)   Mt 5:9
(9)   Lk 1:51, 52
(10) Lk 1:52
(11) Jas 1:9-11, 17

Suffering

Suffering is part of every human life. When united with the suffering of Christ, it becomes his suffering today. It is growthful, forming and transforming. This is especially true when it is suffering for the cause of right.

 God, the sufferings of your Son overflow into our lives.
So too does the encouragement we receive through
  him.[1]

There are times, God, when I am tempted to
    despair like Paul,
when my suffering overwhelms me.[2]

Your Son, Jesus, committed no sin,
yet he endured all the hardships that mortals can
    suffer,
leaving me an example.[3]

In Gethsemane he felt sadness to the point of death.
He understands me now in my fear of suffering.[4]

Deepen in me the unseen mystery that good can
    come from suffering.
In this revelation give me perseverance like your
    prophets of old.[5]

My present sufferings are nothing compared with
    my glory yet to come,
when what is mortal will be clothed in immortality
and death will be swallowed up in victory.[6]

Let me never believe that my suffering is your
    punishment for sin,
since doing what is right can lead to suffering too.[7]

≈

Strengthen me, God, with the strength of Christ,
as I share with others the hardships of life.[8]

≈

By your grace I can rejoice in my suffering,
for suffering brings perseverance, character and hope
– a hope that can never be disappointed, that can
    never fade away,
because your love has been poured into my heart
    by the Holy Spirit.[9]

≈

Mold me through suffering into the pattern of
    Christ's death.
May I come to know the power of his resurrection.[10]

≈

May you, my God, the God of all grace,
restore, confirm and strengthen me
when my sufferings are over.
To you be eternal dominion for ever. Amen.[11]

References

(1)	2 Cor 1:5	(2)	2 Cor 1:8-11
(3)	Heb 4:15 & 2:18	(4)	Mt 26:38
(5)	Phil 1:12-14 & 1 Thess 2:14, 15		
(6)	Rom 8:18-21 & 1 Cor 15:53-58		
(7)	Jn 9:1-3 & 1 Pet 3:17	(8)	Phil 4:13-19
(9)	Rom 5:3-5 & 1 Pet 1:3, 4	(10)	Phil 3:8-11
(11)	1 Pet 5:10, 11		

*T*emptation

Temptation is an inclination to selfishness and sin, which will always be part of our lives.

 I pray, God, that I may be rooted in faith
and not fall away in times of testing.[1]

Your Son Jesus was tempted by what he suffered.
He helps those who are now being tested.[2]

Just as I share in the sufferings of Christ,
I will shout for joy when his glory is revealed.[3]

Preserve me, God, from the hour of trial.
May I keep your word of patient endurance.[4]

I approach with boldness your throne of grace
to receive mercy and grace in my time of need.[5]

Let me not use my power for self-indulgence
nor tempt my God to prove myself,
following not evil to gain worldly power.
Away with such things – I worship you, God.[6]

Protect me with your power as I suffer various trials.
Make genuine my faith – more precious than gold.
Bring it to praise and glory.[7]

Strengthen my endurance when faith is tested.
Bring me to maturity and completeness
– lacking in nothing.[8]

～

When my mission, with its temptations to give up,
    is ended,
may I bow my head and surrender my spirit,
praying with Jesus: 'It is finished.'[9]
'Into your hands I commend my spirit.'[10]

References

(1)	Lk 8:13	(2)	Heb 2:18
(3)	1 Pet 4:12, 13	(4)	Rev 3:10-12
(5)	Heb 4:15, 16	(6)	Mt 4:1-11
(7)	1 Pet 1:3-7	(8)	Jas 1:2-4
(9)	Jn 19:30	(10)	Lk 23:46

*T*rinity

The word is not found in the scriptures, but the Gospels and Epistles tell us of the three Persons with their individual attributes and work.

 Father, in the beginning was the Word
and the Word was with you.[1]
You loved him in the Spirit
before the foundation of the world.[2]

Your Son shared in the glory of your presence
before ever the world began.[3]

He is the reflection of your own glory
and the exact imprint of your very being.[4]

This only Son who is close to your heart,
he alone sees you and makes you known.[5]

In the presence of the Spirit,
you identified your beloved Son,
with whom you are well pleased.[6]

Yes, Father, through the Spirit you love your Son
and entrust everything into his hands,[7]
and show him all you are doing.[8]

You know your Son and your Son knows you,
and all that you have is his.[9]

In love, in the Spirit,
you show him all that you are doing.[10]

≈

You filled him with the joy of the Holy Spirit
and he blessed your precious revelation to the
    world.[11]

≈

Glory to you Father; I am your child.
Glory to you the Son; you are my brother.
Glory to you Holy Spirit; you are my life.[12]

≈

With the spirit of love, a community of love,
three persons in love, you, God, are love.[13]

References

(1)   Jn 1:1   (2)   Jn 17:24
(3)   Jn 17:5   (4)   Heb 1:3
(5)   Jn 1:18 & 10:30   (6)   Mk 1:9-11
(7)   Jn 3:32-35   (8)   Jn 5:20
(9)   Jn 10:15 & 17:10   (10) Jn 5:20
(11) Lk 10:21, 22   (12) Jn 16:26, 27 & 20:17 & Gal 4:6, 7
(13) 1 Jn 4:8

*T**ruth***

In scripture, truth is that which is genuine, certain and powerful. God is Truth itself and Jesus is 'full of grace and truth.'

 Your Word, God, became flesh and lived among us
– full of grace and truth.[1]

Help me to speak the truth in love,
that I may grow up in every way into Christ.[2]

May I never turn away from listening to the truth,
not wandering away to myths,[3]
but living as a child – a child of the light –
fruitful in all that is good, true and right.[4]

Bring to my mind what I learned from Christ.
The Spirit is the truth,
and the truth is in Jesus.[5]

Spirit of God, guide me into all truth.
Declare to me also the things that are to come.[6]

If I continue in the word of Jesus,
I will be truly his disciple.
I will learn the truth
and the truth will set me free.[7]

Gift my heart with a love for the truth,
for refusing to love truth is to perish.[8]

❧

Jesus is the way, the truth and the life.
Sanctify me, God, in the truth.[9]

❧

With Jesus who was born and came into the world,
let me always testify to the truth.[10]

References

(1)	Jn 1:14	(2)	Eph 4:15
(3)	2 Tim 4:3, 4	(4)	Eph 5:8, 9
(5)	Eph 4:19-21 & 1 Jn 5:6	(6)	Jn 16:13
(7)	Jn 8:31, 32	(8)	2 Thess 2:9, 10
(9)	Jn 14:6 & 17:19	(10)	Jn 18:37

*U*nion *with God*

All people are equally loved by God. The purpose of life's journey is to grow through love in union with our God, and our journey ends when this union is complete in heaven.

 I thank you, God, for birthing me anew
through water and the Spirit.[1]

Give me the water that springs forth within,
gushing up to life eternal.[2]

Help me to worship in spirit and in truth,
for you yourself are spirit.[3]

Strengthen my faith in the one you have sent.
May his word abide in me.[4]

Give to me a believer's heart.
Rivers of living water shall flow.[5]

You abide with me, God;
you are within me.
Deepen my knowing – my awareness.[6]

Jesus is the vine and we the branches.
Nurture my faith in his abiding presence.[7]

May the Spirit guide me into all truth
and your love be poured into my heart.[8]

Protect me in your name, my God,
that, as Jesus prayed, we may be one.[9]

≈

You will see me again and my heart will rejoice
– a joy that can never be taken away.[10]

References

(1) Jn 3:3-7

(2) Jn 4:14

(3) Jn 4:24

(4) Jn 5:37, 38

(5) Jn 7:37-39

(6) Jn 14:19, 20

(7) Jn 15:4, 5

(8) Jn 16:12-14 & Rom 5:5

(9) Jn 17:11

(10) Jn 16:22

*V*ictory

Our victory is being won as we become more united to God and his people by the power of the Holy Spirit. It will be complete in heaven.

With Jesus, I lift up my eyes to God
and give thanks for the hearing of my prayers.
I know God hears me always.[1]

Thanks to God for my faith, through Jesus,
empowering my love of all God's people
because of the hope stored up for me in heaven.[2]

May the peace of Christ reign in my heart
for this is our calling as one,[3]
joyful at all times and constant in prayer.
This is your plan, God, for me, in Christ Jesus.[4]

From the riches of your glory, you fulfill all my
    needs.
To you is glory forever.[5]

I know that whoever is born of God
and whoever believes in his Son
has victory over the world.[6]

While my life is being poured away
and when the time to depart comes near,
may the crown of righteousness be mine.[7]

When my body puts on immortality,
death too will be swallowed up in victory,
and then I can say 'Where, O death, is your
    victory?
Where, O death, is your sting?'[8]

❧

Sanctify me, God, and keep me blameless.
You are the One who is faithful.[9]

❧

Thanks to you for giving me the victory,
through Jesus Christ, my Savior.[10]

References

(1) Jn 11:41,42   (2) Col 1:3-5
(3) Col 3:15   (4) 1 Thess 5:16-18
(5) Phil 4:19   (6) 1 Jn 5:4, 5
(7) 2 Tim 4:6-8   (8) 1 Cor 15:52-56
(9) 1 Thess 5:23, 24   (10) 1 Cor 15:57

Waiting

We wait with patience for the final coming and revelation of Jesus, at our own death and at the end of the world.

 As I wait for the fullness of my adoption,
the redemption of my body,
gift me anew, God, with the fruit of your Spirit.[1]

With inward groaning and through the spirit of
faith,
I eagerly wait for the hope of righteousness.[2]

Help me to bear fruit with patient endurance,
holding fast to the word with honesty and
goodness.[3]

Like Simeon looking forward to Israel's
consolation,
strengthen my waiting and deepen my hope.[4]

Mold my life into holiness and godliness
as I wait for and hasten the coming of your day.[5]

When I meet persecution, when troubles arise,
make patient my waiting,
make strong my endurance.[6]

Ready me to wait like the Baptist, John.
I know you will come when we least expect.[7]

To those who experience the pain of waiting,
let me show the compassion of Jesus.[8]

≈

Because the testimony to Christ
was confirmed among us,
I do not lack any spiritual gift
as I eagerly await his final revelation.[9]

≈

Like the apostles, in unity and prayer-filled hope
let me wait for the fulfillment of the Father's
    promise.[10]

References

(1)	Rom 8:22, 23	(2)	Gal 5:5
(3)	Lk 8:15	(4)	Lk 2:29-32
(5)	2 Pet 3:11, 12	(6)	Mk 4:17
(7)	Mt 11:3 & 24:50	(8)	Mk 8:2
(9)	1 Cor 1:6, 7	(10)	Acts 1:4

*W*ater

In scripture, water symbolizes life, refreshment, cleansing and the abundance of divine blessings.

 God, through the guiding power of your spirit,
lead me to springs of the water of life.[1]

Give to me this water in abundance.
I who am thirsty wish to come to you.[2]

The water you give will become a spring
gushing up to eternal life.[3]

Help me to believe in Jesus more deeply.
Whoever believes will never be thirsty.[4]

Gift every person with a believer's heart.
Rivers of living water shall flow.[5]

Cleanse our world and touch it with healing.
Make me generous in reaching out.[6]

Jesus, you used water for the first of your signs
revealing your glory while meeting a need.[7]

You turned water into wine
to gladden the human heart.[8]

PRAYING THE NEW TESTAMENT AS PSALMS

Like a slave, you washed the apostles' feet,
showing with water God's love for us all.[9]

꩜

Be with me as I walk over the waters of life.
Let me hear your words: 'It is I, take heart.'[10]

꩜

The water of life, God, clear as crystal,
flows from your throne and the throne of the
    Lamb.[11]

References

(1)   Rev 7:17   (2)   Rev 22:17
(3)   Jn 4:14   (4)   Jn 6:35
(5)   Jn 7:37-39   (6)   Jn 5:6-9
(7) (8) Jn 2:1-12   (9)   Jn 13:3-5
(10) Mk 6:47-52   (11) Rev 22:1

Weakness

God understands and accepts our weak moments and asks us to be patient with our own frailties and with the weaknesses of others.

 God, I know that my flesh is weak,
but my spirit indeed is willing.[1]

Help me to accept my limitations.
You choose what is weak to shame the strong.[2]

Jesus, your Son, was crucified in weakness
but lives by your power, the power of God.[3]

You will always provide sufficient of your grace,
for power is made perfect in weakness.
Let me boast of my weaknesses, knowing
     contentment,
for when I am weak, then I am strong.[4]

Ready me to welcome those weak in faith,
putting up with their failings, not pleasing myself.[5]

For at the right time, when we were still weak,
your Son Jesus died for us, the ungodly.[6]

For the sake of the Gospel, I become weak to the
     weak,
all things to all people, to win some at least.[7]

Your weakness, God, is stronger than my strength;
your foolishness above human wisdom.
I want to know Jesus, the crucified Christ,
knowing his power at work in my weakness.[8]

≈

I await with longing the resurrection of the dead,
when what is perishable becomes imperishable
and what is sown in weakness is raised in power.[9]

≈

Though afflicted but not crushed,
perplexed but not despairing,
I own that the power belongs to you, God.
Be with me in my weakness.[10]

References

(1)	Mt 26:41	(2)	Rom 6:19 & 1 Cor 1:27
(3)	2 Cor 13:3, 4	(4)	2 Cor 12:8-10
(5)	Rom 14:1 & 15:1	(6)	Rom 5:6
(7)	1 Cor 9:22, 23	(8)	1 Cor 1:20-25
(9)	1 Cor 15:42, 43	(10)	2 Cor 4:7-11

Wisdom

Wisdom – Sophia – is the radiant and unfading guidance of God. She is readily perceived by those who love her and found by those who seek her.

 God, you have made foolish the wisdom of the
     world;
the world lacked the wisdom to know you.[1]

So we proclaim the Gospel, not with eloquence
but with the crucified Christ
– your power and your wisdom.[2]

You have chosen us, God – the foolish in the
     world,
chosen us in Christ to shame the wise.[3]

May my faith never rest on human wisdom
but on the power of your spirit
– the spirit of Christ Jesus.[4]

Open my heart ever more deeply,
as I speak in words not humanly taught
but taught by your Spirit to those who are
     spiritual.[5]

Prepare me to become a fool that I may become
     wise,
for the wisdom of this world is foolishness to you.[6]

Gift me with grace and godly sincerity,
that earthly wisdom may not be my boast.[7]

⁓

In all spiritual wisdom and understanding, God,
fill me with the knowledge of your will,
that I may lead a life worthy of you,
bearing fruit in every good work.[8]

⁓

Keep me from envy and selfish ambition.
Grace me with gentleness born of wisdom.[9]

⁓

I confess my lacking in wisdom, God,
but in faith, never doubting,
I ask you to fill me.[10]

References

(1) (2) (3) 1 Cor 1:17-31 (4) (5) 1 Cor 2:6-13
(6) 1 Cor 3:18-20 (7) 2 Cor 1:12
(8) Col 1:9, 10 (9) Jas 3:13-15
(10) Jas 1:5, 6

*W*itness

We witness for God when we make God visible by the goodness of our lives,
even to death, as Jesus did.

 And a voice from heaven said:
'This is my Son, the Beloved,
with whom I am well pleased.'[1]

Yes, God, the work that Jesus did
testified that you had sent him.
Be with me in my mission as I witness to the
truth.[2]

Your Spirit is the one that testifies.
I know the Spirit is truth.[3]

Nourish in my heart the faith you have given
– eternal life in Jesus your Son.[4]

Jesus, you are the faithful witness,
the origin of God's creation.
For this you were born and came into the world
– to testify to the truth.[5]

Like those who witnessed Christ's death and his
rising
let me, God, be a witness to all,[6]
by the word of my testimony, even to death,
and in the power of your spirit,
by the blood of the Lamb.[7]

PRAYING THE NEW TESTAMENT AS PSALMS

With John, let me testify to Jesus, the light.
He enlightens the hearts of all who receive him.[8]

≈

Thank you, God, for the gift of the scriptures,
testifying to Jesus and giving me life.[9]

≈

Let me testify to all the Word
whom I have seen and heard.
Then my joy will be complete
as together we share in fellowship
with you our Father.[10]

References

(1)	Mt 3:17	(2)	Jn 5:36
(3)	1 Jn 5:6	(4)	1 Jn 5:10,11
(5)	Rev 1:4, 5 & 3:14 & Jn 18:37		
(6)	Lk 24:46, 47 & Acts 22:14, 15		
(7)	Rev 12:11 & Acts 1:8	(8)	Jn 1:6-9
(9)	Jn 5:39	(10)	1 Jn 1:1-4

*W*oman

God chose to become wonderfully manifest in the lives of many women in the Old and New Testaments. Christ upheld the dignity of women, among whom were many of his followers. They stayed with him to the end, stood by the cross at his death and were the first to proclaim his resurrection.

 God, when the fullness of time had come,
you sent your Son, born of a woman.[1]

Truly Mary is blessed among women,
and blessed is the fruit of her womb.[2]

As with Elizabeth, gift mothers with the fullness of
    your Spirit.
Let the children within them leap for joy.[3]

With Anna the prophet let me speak about Jesus.
Deepen my spirit of prayer and fasting.[4]

Bring me to willingly share of my plenty,
remembering the poor widow who offered her all.[5]

May I sit at the feet of Jesus, like Mary,
listening to him in the home of my heart.[6]

Like the sinful woman, knowing deeply the joy of
    forgiveness,
make me great, God, in showing my love.[7]

Give me the faith of the Canaanite woman,
who trusted totally when all seemed lost.[8]

Gift me with courage and compassion,
like the women on Calvary – loyal to the end.[9]

References

(1) Gal 4:4   (2) Lk 1:42
(3) Lk 1:41, 42   (4) Lk 2:36-38
(5) Mk 12:41-44   (6) Lk 10:38-42
(7) Lk 7:36-50   (8) Mt 15:21-28
(9) Mt 27:55-61

Word

Jesus is the Word because he is the complete manifestation of the Father. He also spoke the word of God, which has the power to transform us insofar as we are open to accept it.

'In the beginning was the Word
and the Word was with God
and the Word was God.'[1]

'And the Word became flesh
and lived among us.'
May I proclaim what I have seen and heard
concerning the Word of life.[2]

God, your word is truth.
Cleanse me by the word
and sanctify me in the truth.[3]

Give me grace to keep your word
and then I shall never see death.
Deepen my love and make me faithful.
Your words are spirit and life.[4]

Jesus, you spoke as God commanded you.
May everyone believe in your word.[5]

With Peter, we ask 'To whom can we go?
You have the words of eternal life.'[6]

May I always remember your death and your rising,
the scripture and the word that you have spoken.[7]

∼

Fill my heart, God, with total acceptance
and a deep understanding of your word.[8]

∼

Gift me with ready obedience to your word
that your love in me may reach perfection.
In you I abide. Let me walk like Jesus.
I want to be found in him.[9]

References

(1) Jn 1:1   (2) Jn 1:14 & 1 Jn 1:1-3
(3) Jn 15:3 & 17:17   (4) Jn 8:51 & 14:24 & 6:63
(5) Jn 12:48-50 & 4:41   (6) Jn 6:68
(7) Jn 2:22   (8) Jn 8:43
(9) 1 Jn 2:5, 6

Worship

Worship is an expression of our reverence before the infinite and awesome grandeur of God.

 Let me worship my God in spirit and in truth.
The time for true worship is here.[1]

❧

You ask us, God, to worship thus,
for you are spirit and truth.[2]

❧

Draw my heart ever closer to you,
that I may worship in sincerity and faith.[3]

❧

Make yourself known to all in our world.
Help me in proclaiming your word.[4]

❧

You made the world and everything in it.
You are the God of heaven and earth.[5]

❧

You do not depend on our work or service
for you give life and breath to all things.[6]

❧

With conscience clear, I worship my God,
day and night remembering all people in prayer.[7]

❧

In faith, let me turn to the law and the prophets,
worshipping always the God of my ancestors.[8]

❧

With the joy of the women on Easter morn,
may I fall at the feet of Jesus in worship.[9]

And when I am called to the mountaintop,
let me worship in total, unquestioning faith.[10]

References

(1)	Jn 4:23	(2)	Jn 4:23, 24
(3)	Mt 15:7-9	(4) (5) (6)	Acts 17:23-25
(7)	2 Tim 1:3	(8)	Acts 24:14
(9)	Mt 28:9	(10)	Mt 28:16, 17

Index of Bible Verses

(Each verse or passage is followed by the page numbers where it is cited.)

Matthew
1:14, 21 ....**111**
1:16, 17 ....**110**
1:18-22...............**110**
1:18-25...............**140**
1:19. 20 ....**110**
1:22, 23 ....**110**
2:10 ....**114**
2:13-15...............**111**
2:19-23..........**75, 111**
3:2 ....**108**
3:7, 8 ....**84**
3:8 ....**108**
3:17 ....**204**
4:1-4 ....**30**
4:1-11 ....**186**
4:13-16...............**121**
4:18-20...............**154**
4:18-22...............**140**
4:23 ....**116**
5:3 ....**14**
5:4 ....**14**
5:5 ....**14**
5:6 ....**14, 182**
5:7 ....**14, 137**
5:8 ....**14**
5:9 ....**14, 82,
150, 183**
5:10 ....**14**
5:11 ....**15**
5:12 ....**15**
5:13 ....**62**
5:14-16...............**123**
5:44, 45...........**63, 79**
5:48 ....**136**
6:9 ....**98**
6:9, 10 ....**115**
6:12-15...............**79**
6:25-33...............**156**
6:28-30...............**62**
6:30-31...............**70**
7:7-11 ....**159**
7:15-20...............**85**
7:29 ....**22**
8:1-4...............**138**
8:5-8...............**94**
8:5-13...............**139**
8:9 ....**144**
8:16, 17 ....**94**
9:1-8...........**95, 138**
9:18-26...............**138**

9:36 ....**42**
10:16 ....**180**
11:3 ....**196**
11:4 ....**124**
11:10 ....**108**
11:28-30...............**60**
11:29 ....**47**
12:9-14...............**139**
12:46-50...............**30**
13:10, 11 ....**29**
13:13-18...............**95**
13:14, 15 ....**124**
13:31, 32 ....**28**
13:32, 33 ....**62**
13:33 ....**62**
13:43 ....**28**
13:44 ....**29, 62**
14:4-12...............**108**
14:13-21...............**138**
14:22-23...............**138**
14:28-33...............**154**
15:7-9 ....**210**
15:21-28...............**207**
15:22-28...............**139**
15:30, 31 ....**94**
16:21-23...............**154**
16:24-25...............**164**
17:1-4 ....**154**
17:2 ....**122**
17:14-20...............**138**
18:1-4...............**181**
18:2-4...............**117**
18:3, 4 ....**166**
18:21, 22 ....**136**
19:4-6...............**130**
19:16-22...............**57**
19:21 ....**116**
20:19 ....**45**
20:20-22...............**142**
20:25-28...............**118**
20:29-34...............**138**
21:28-31...............**74**
21:43 ....**84**
22:1, 2 ....**74**
24:50 ....**196**
25:33-40...............**127**
25:34 ....**29**
25:34, 35 ....**104**
26:27, 28 ....**68**
26:28 ....**44**
26:38 ....**184**

26:39 ....**44, 62**
26:40, 41 ....**154**
26:41...............**44, 200**
26:42 ....**113**
26:49, 50 ....**174**
26:50 ....**82**
26:51,52,67 ....**30**
26:69-75...............**155**
27:14 ....**44**
27:24 ....**44**
27:46 ....**44, 95**
27:51-53...............**44**
27:55-61...............**207**
27:56.....**45, 128, 142**
28:9 ....**211**
28:16, 17 ....**211**
28:18 ....**22**
28:20 ....**61**

Mark
1:9-11 ....**188**
1:14, 15 ....**166**
1:41 ....**46**
2:5-8 ....**25**
2:10 ....**22**
2:23-28...............**30**
3:14-15...............**22**
4:17 ....**196**
4:31, 32 ....**62**
4:39, 40 ....**62**
5:19 ....**82**
5:25, 26 ....**94**
6:30-31...............**174**
6:31, 32 ....**135**
6:34 ....**36**
6:47-52...............**199**
7:24-30...............**142**
8:2 ....**197**
8:35 ....**172**
9:1 ....**28**
9:7 ....**124**
9:36 ....**25**
9:50 ....**150**
10:6 ....**96**
10:21, 22 ....**154**
11:25 ....**79**
12:41-44...............**206**
12:43, 44 ....**156**
13:13 ....**67**
14:7 ....**154**
14:22-25...............**104**

14:24 ....**50**
16:14, 15 ....**140**

Luke
1:25 ....**143**
1:26-35...............**132**
1:31 ....**24**
1:32, 33 ....**28**
1:35...............**101, 142**
1:38 ....**140**
1:39-45...............**132**
1:41, 42 ....**206**
1:42 ....**206**
1:43, 44 ....**114**
1:46, 47 ....**114**
1:50 ....**136**
1:51, 52 ....**183**
1:52 ....**183**
1:68, 69 ....**51,
164, 172**
1:70-74 ....**51**
1:76-78...........**46, 136,
137,162**
1:77 ....**172**
2:4-7 ....**110**
2:6, 7 ....**24**
2:7 ....**62**
2:8-20 ....**43**
2:10, 11 ....**114**
2:13, 14 ....**86**
2:15, 16 ....**110**
2:21 ....**110**
2:22-24...............**110**
2:27 ....**100**
2:29-32...............**196**
2:30-32...............**122**
2:33-35...............**142**
2:34, 35 ....**133**
2:36-38...............**206**
2:40 ....**132**
2:42-52...............**132**
2:52 ....**131**
3:21, 22 ....**38**
4:1, 2 ....**25**
4:5-8 ....**30**
4:17, 18 ....**140**
4:18 ....**100, 156, 166**
5:4-8...............**154**
5:15, 16 ....**38**
5:29...............**25, 134**
6:11, 12 ....**38**

Luke (cont.)
6:20..............12, 156
6:21 12
6:22 12
6:22, 23 20
6:23 12
6:24 12
6:25 12
6:26 13
6:27, 28 16
6:27-31 13
6:36 162
7:11-15 142
7:13 46
7:36-50.......135, 206
8:1, 2 128
8:13 186
8:15 196
8:40-42 74
9:1, 2 ....60, 94
9:12-17 134
9:28-36 87
9:46-48 180
9:58 ....25, 174
10:21 ....20, 101
10:21, 22 189
10:29-37 104
10:38 130
10:38-42 206
11:1 60
11:1-4 ....38, 158
11:5, 8 38
11:5-8 94
11:9-13 94
11:11-13 74
12:12 100
12:15 156
12:22-31 18
12:32 116
13:29 104
13:31, 32 174
13:34 142
14:16-21 105
14:33 60
15:6 82
15:11-13 74
15:11-32 163
17:4 136
17:11-14 93
18:1 66
18:15, 16 142
19:5-10 30
19:6 104
19:41 24
21:1-4............56, 57
21:18, 19 66

22:14-20 134
22:19 68
22: 31, 32 38
22:34 79
22:41, 42 39
22:42 ....36, 145
22:48 82
23:42, 43 28
23:44, 45 63
23:46 187
24:3 128
24:11 128
24:28-32 105
24:30, 31 135
24:41-43 134
24:43, 46 95
24:46, 47 204
24:47 166

John
1:1........40, 188, 208
1:1-3.............27, 208
1:2, 3 40
1:4-9 26
1:4-13 32
1:6-8 108
1:6-9 205
1:7, 21 26
1:12 ....23, 32
1:14 ...18, 24, 26, 33,
    62, 132, 190, 208
1:18 188
1:19-23 140
1:23 109
1:23, 29 108
1:27 109
1:33, 34 109
2:1, 2 25
2:1-11........132, 134
2:1-12 198
2:22 ....70, 209
3:3-7 192
3:16 88
3:31, 32 41
3:32-34 26
3:32-35 188
3:34-36 70
3:36 178
4:6 25
4:7-14 134
4:9 174
4:14.............192, 198
4:23 210
4:23, 24 210
4:24 192
4:25, 26 32

4:27 30
4:34 ....36, 144
4:41 208
5:6-9 198
5:20 ....112, 188, 189
5:24 ....32, 169
5:26, 27 22
5:30 ....22, 145
5:35 108
5:36 204
5:36-38 33
5:37, 38 58,
        70, 192
5:39 205
6:15 174
6:27 68
6:35........68, 69, 198
6:37-39 69
6:38-40.........37, 144
6:40 37
6:49, 50 68
6:51 68
6:54 69
6:55, 56 69
6:63 208
6:66, 67 30
6:66-69 154
6:67-69 141
6:68 208
7:17 144
7:28, 29 26
7:29 112
7:37-39........192, 198
8:28 ....26, 36
8:28, 29 145
8:29 ....36, 112
8:31, 32........60, 190
8:31-36 81
8:34-36 179
8:43 209
8:46 175
8:47 58
8:50 32
8:51 208
8:54 113
8:58 40
9:1-3 185
10:4 42
10:10 ....23, 42
10:11 ....42, 88
10:14, 15 42
10:15 188
10:16 42
10:17, 18.....168, 174
10:18 31
10:30 188

10:37-38 32
11:3 128
11:5 25
11:24-26 106
11:25, 26 120
11:41, 42 194
11:42, 43 112
12:1, 2 134
12:24-26 56
12:27-28 27
12:28 87
12:35, 36 122
12:46 122
12:48-50 208
13:3-5 199
13:12-15 118
13:13, 14 60
13:34 126
13:34, 35 60
13:35 126
14:1, 27 95
14:6.............26, 191
14:7-9 26
14:9, 10 27
14:11 32
14:13 159
14:19, 20 192
14:24 208
14:27 151
14:28 20
14:31..........113, 145
15:3 208
15:4, 5 192
15:5 85
15:9 88
15:11 21
15:12, 13 88
15:13 126
16:5-7 20
16:8, 9 178
16:12-14 192
16:13 190
16:14 32
16:22 193
16:24 20
16:26, 27 189
16:28 112
17:2 22
17:4 ....36, 145
17:5 188
17:6 33
17:9 88
17:10 188
17:11...........38, 193
17:15 39
17:17 208

John (cont.)
17:19 ....**191**
17:21, 22 ....**176**
17: 21-23 ....**39**
17:24............**113, 188**
17:25, 26 ....**112**
18:36, 37 ....**28**
18:37.....**32, 191, 204**
19:23, 24 ....**133**
19:25..........**129, 142**
19:26, 27.....**132, 174**
19:30............**54, 187**
20:1 ....**128**
20:15 ....**129**
20:16 ....**128**
20:17 ....**189**
20:18 ....**128**
21:3 ....**63**
21:3-11 ....**135**

Acts of the Apostles
1:4 ....**197**
1:8 ....**100, 204**
1:14 ....**131**
1:22 ....**168**
1:24 ....**96**
2:17-21 ....**124**
2:23, 24 ....**168**
2:42.............**52, 158**
2:44, 45 ....**57**
3:6, 7 ....**155**
3:19, 20 ....**167**
4:31 ....**100**
4:32 ....**126**
5:15, 16 ....**94**
5:31 ....**166**
7:55 ....**101**
8: 15, 17 ....**101**
9:5 ....**148**
9:31 ....**100**
10:31 ....**159**
11:23, 24 ....**96**
12:6-11 ....**155**
13:52 ....**100**
14:22 ....**64**
15:30, 31 ....**64**
15:31 ....**64**
16:40 ....**65**
17:23-25 ....**210**
17:24-28 ....**91**
17:30 ....**167**
18:27 ....**65**
20:22 ....**100**
20:32 ....**98**
24:14 ....**210**
22:14, 15 ....**204**

24:16 ....**48**
26:18 ....**166**

Romans
1:3-5 ....**124**
1:11-12 ....**148**
1:11-13 ....**84**
1:17 ....**120**
1:18-21 ....**91**
1:25 ....**17**
2:1-7 ....**147**
2:4 ....**96**
2:4, 5 ....**167**
3:23, 24 ....**86**
3:24 ....**81**
4:18 ....**102**
5:1, 2..........**102, 150**
5:3-5 ....**185**
5:5..........**88, 94, 192**
5:6 ....**200**
5:7 ....**88**
5:9 ....**172**
5:10 ....**162**
5:20 ....**78, 163**
6:1, 2 ....**179**
6:3, 4 ....**121**
6:3-6 ....**169**
6:4, 5 ....**76, 86**
6:6, 7 ....**178**
6:8-11 ....**77**
6:10-11 ....**121**
6:12, 13 ....**18, 178**
6:16 ....**178**
6:19 ....**200**
6:22 ....**178**
7:4 ....**84**
7:22-25 ....**179**
8:11 ....**106, 120**
8:17 ....**53**
8:18-21 ....**184**
8:21 ....**81**
8:22, 23 ....**196**
8:24 ....**172**
8:24, 25 ....**102**
8:26, 27 ....**158**
8:27 ....**96**
8:28 ....**25**
9:1 ....**49**
9:4, 5 ....**50**
9:19-21 ....**22**
10:16, 17 ....**124**
11:33 ....**90**
11:34, 35 ....**90**
11:36 ....**91**
12:1 ....**99, 170**
12:2 ....**58**

12:6-20 ....**104**
12:12, 14 ....**20**
12:13 ....**158**
12:15 ....**25, 127**
13:5 ....**48**
14:1 ....**200**
14:7 ....**115**
14:7-9 ....**120**
14:17 ....**116, 150**
14:19 ....**150**
15:1 ....**200**
15:4 ....**102**
15:5, 6 ....**67**
15:7 ....**127**
15:13 ....**102,
                   115, 150**
15:25-27 ....**156**
15:30, 32 ....**82**
16:1-23 ....**82**
16:25-27 ....**34**

1 Corinthians
1:4, 5 ....**92**
1:6, 7 ....**197**
1:9 ....**76**
1:17-31 ....**202**
1:20-25 ....**201**
1:22-24 ....**152**
1:27 ....**200**
2:6-13 ....**202**
2:9-11 ....**34**
2:14-15 ....**59**
3:16, 17 ....**18**
3:18-20 ....**202**
4:1 ....**34**
4:1, 2 ....**118**
4:4 ....**48**
5:6-8 ....**180**
5:7, 8 ....**170**
6:11 ....**99**
6:19, 20 ....**18**
7:15 ....**150**
7:21, 22 ....**80**
8:4-6 ....**90**
8:6 ....**74**
8:8, 9 ....**80**
9:19-23 ....**148**
9:22 ....**176**
9:22, 23 ....**77, 201**
9:24-27 ....**56**
10:13 ....**152**
10:16 ....**16**
10:16, 17 ....**76, 176**
11:12 ....**130**
12:4-11 ....**126**
12:9, 28 ....**94**

13:4 ....**146**
13:4-8 ....**126**
13:6 ....**20**
13:13 ....**126**
14:3 ....**64**
14:33 ....**150**
15:3-5 ....**168**
15:19-22 ....**106**
15:20 ....**168**
15:39-54 ....**54**
15:42, 43 ......**87, 201**
15:42-54 ....**19**
15:52-56 ....**195**
15:53-58 ....**184**
15:54, 55 ....**106**
15:57 ....**195**
16:20 ....**99**

2 Corinthians
1:3 ....**78**
1:3, 4 ....**16**
1:4 ....**152**
1:5 ....**107, 184**
1:7 ....**153**
1:8-11 ....**184**
1:11 ....**159**
1:12 ....**180, 181, 203**
1:19, 20 ....**50**
1:24 ....**20**
2:14 ....**93**
2:17 ....**180**
3:4-6 ....**50**
3:17 ....**80**
3:18 ....**161**
4:4-6 ....**123**
4:6 ....**141**
4:7-11 ....**201**
4:10 ....**148**
4:16-18 ....**56**
5:1 ....**55**
5:1-3 ....**149**
5:11 ....**48**
5:17-6:1 ....**163**
6:11-13 ....**181**
6:14 ....**76**
7:3 ....**76**
8:3, 4 ....**176**
8:23 ....**53**
9:7, 8 ....**16, 17**
9:7-9 ....**156**
9:10-12 ....**92**
10:8 ....**119**
11:2, 3 ....**180**
11:3 ....**161**
11:13, 14 ....**181**
12:8-10 ....**200**

PRAYING THE NEW TESTAMENT AS PSALMS

2 Corinthians (cont.)
13:3, 4 200
13:13 ....77, 176

Galatians
2:20 ....107, 165
3:13, 14 164
3:16 50
4:4 206
4:6, 7 189
5:1 80
5:5 196
5:13 80
5:22 ....88, 114
5:22-23 84

Ephesians
1:3 16
1:3, 4 50
1:7, 8 78
1:7-11 35
1:13, 14 172
2:4, 5 ....52, 106
2:4-6 89
2:5-9 173
2:13 50
2:14 150
2:15-18 150
3:3 34
3:9 34
3:14, 15 74
3:16-19 127
3:17 96
3:19 89
4:1-3 146
4:4-6 75
4:15 190
4:19-21 190
4:22-24 56
4:31 78
4:32 78
5:1, 2 170
5:2 171
5:5 28
5:8 123
5:8, 9 190
5:10-17 58
5:11 76
5:17 58
5:19, 20 93
5:25 130
5:25-33 73
5:32 131
5:33 130
6:10-17 56
6:18 158

Philippians
1:3 148
1:7 53
1:8 ....47, 52
1:12-14 184
1:20 ....19, 54
1:22-23 85
1:23 54
1:29 71
2:5-7 24
2:5-8 144
2:5-9 36
2:6-8 41
2:20 83
3:7-9 57
3:8 149
3:8-11 185
3:10 ....53, 177
3:10, 11 169
3:12-16 148
3:20, 221 172
4:4 20
4:6, 7 92
4:13-19 185
4:15 52
4:16, 17 85
4:19 ....171, 194

Colossians
1:3, 14, 17 117
1:3-5 194
1:9, 10 ....58, 203
1:11-12 146
1:11-14 122
1:13, 14 137,
                    162, 165
1:15, 16 40
1:17, 19 40
1:18 166
1:19, 20 ......162, 164
1:21-23 162
1:24-26 118
1:26, 27 102
1:27 34
1:28 34
2:2, 3 35
2:6, 7 92
2:9 18
2:12 168
3:2-4 121
3:12 46
3:12, 13 147
3:13 136
3:15 ....150, 194
3:16 16
3:19 130

3:20 72
3:21 ....72, 75
4:3, 4 35
4:10, 11 82
4:12 59

1 Thessalonians
1:6 115
2:13 125
2:14, 15 184
3:7-9 92
3:13 98
4:7, 8 160
4:13, 14 55
4:14 70
4:17, 18 52
5:4-8 160
5:14 147
5:15 78
5:16, 17 20
5:16-18 194
5:23 ....18, 150
5:23, 24 195

2 Thessalonians
1:4 67
1:4, 5 152
1:11 117
2:9, 10 191
2:13 94
2:16, 17 103
3:1, 2 158
3:5 66

1 Timothy
1:16 147
1:19 48
2:1, 2 158
3:9 48
3:16 34
4:4, 5 ....92, 158
5:8 72
6:6-10 56
6:11 67
6:12 121
6:13-16 28
6:15 90
6:16 ....90, 120

2 Timothy
1:3 ....48, 83, 210
1:4 72
1:5 143
1:8-10 161
2:10-12 66
2:11, 12 152

2: 11-13 177
2:13 70
2:24-26 119
3:13-15 61
4:1-5 119
4:2 64
4:3, 4 190
4:6-7 54
4:6-8 ...140, 149, 194
4:8 ....55, 107

Titus
1:1-4 148
1:8 118
2:3-6 72
2:4, 5 72
2:6 72

Philemon
v. 6 ....52, 177
v. 7 64
v. 20 97

Hebrews
1:3 ....86, 188
1:3, 4 40
2:11 98
2:16-18 24
2:18 ....184, 186
3:8-10 124
3:13 64
3:14 64
4:1, 2 124
4:15 184
4:15, 16 24,
                    163, 186
5:2 24
5:7, 8 145
6:5, 6 164
6:11, 12 146
6:18-20 103
8:10 96
9:13, 14 160
9:15 50
9:26 170
10:5-10 ....36, 144
10:10 ....36, 99
10:22 19
11:1-3 70
11:8 71
11:8, 9 17
12:2 164
12:7 74
12:11 84
12:28 116
13:1-3 105

Hebrews (cont.)
13:4 ....**130**
13:15 ....**171**
13:16..........**170, 176**
13:20, 21........**59, 87**

James
1:2-4 ....**187**
1:5, 6 ....**203**
1:9-11, 17...........**183**
1:12 ....**66**
2:1-4 ....**182**
2:5.............**116, 157**
2:5, 6 ....**182**
2:15-17...............**182**
3:13-15 ....**203**
3:17.............**84, 182**
3:18 ....**182**
4:8 ....**160**
5:1-6 ....**183**
5:7-11 ....**146**
5:11 ....**46, 66**
5:13-16........**94, 158**

1 Peter
1:3..........**54, 95, 120**
1:3-4 ....**185**
1:3-7 ....**186**

1:6-9 ....**55**
1:8, 9..........**114, 173**
1:14-16 ....**98**
1:18, 19 ....**165**
1:22............**125, 160**
2:1-3 ....**181**
2:4, 5 ....**170**
2:9 ....**98, 122**
2:16 ....**80**
2:20, 21 ....**66**
2:20-25 ....**152**
2:21 ....**152**
3:7 ....**130**
3:8 ....**46, 97**
3:11 ....**150**
3:15 ....**48**
3:17 ....**185**
3:18 ....**152**
4:8-10 ....**105**
4:11 ....**86**
4:12, 13 ....**186**
4:12-19 ....**153**
5:1-3 ....**118**
5:3, 4 ....**43**
5:9 ....**56**
5:10, 11 ....**185**
5:14 ....**151**

2 Peter
1:3 ....**91**
1:3, 4 ....**76**
1:4 ....**91, 176**
1:19 ....**96, 103**
2:19, 20 ....**80**
3:8, 9 ....**146**
3:11, 12 ....**196**
3:13 ....**63**
3:13-15 ....**173**

1 John
1:1-3...........**27, 209**
1:1-4 ....**205**
1:3, 4 ....**52**
1:5-7 ....**122**
1:7 ....**160**
1:10 ....**178**
2:5, 6 ....**209**
3:2 ....**87**
3:2, 3..........**102, 160**
3:13, 15 ....**173**
3:17-18 ....**157**
4:8 ....**189**
4:8-10 ....**89**
4:19 ....**166**
5:4, 5 ....**194**
5:6..............**190, 204**

5:10, 11 ....**204**

3 John
v. 4......................**118**

Jude
v. 2......................**151**

Revelation
1:4, 5 ....**204**
2:10 ....**71**
3:10-12 ....**186**
3:14 ....**204**
4:8 ....**98**
5:11-13 ....**17**
5:11-14 ....**41**
7:9, 10 ....**172**
7:12 ....**93**
7:17 ....**198**
12:10 ....**22**
12:11 ....**204**
14:12 ....**66**
19:9 ....**135**
21:22-26 ....**86**
22:1 ....**199**
22:17 ....**198**